To Shirlee
in memory of Muffin
from Mom

Ann Laird

# Where the grass is greener and dogs had better keep off

Ora Spaid

Illustrated by Steve Eberhardt

**L**E

Limited Editions
Milton, Kentucky

Contents of this book may be reproduced in any form provided such reproduction contributes to the welfare of animals and credit is given.

Cover photograph by Pat McDonogh

Guest illustration by Bruce Bolinger

Produced by Digital Printing, Inc., Madison, Indiana


ISBN 0-9649427-0-4

To my dogs, for all they have given me

# Contents

# Prologue

It was easy being a kid when I was one. In the 1920s, kids weren't expected to have good sense; adults did all the thinking. The rules of deportment were simple: pay attention, speak when spoken to and do as you're told. We were not burdened with decisions and when given a choice, it was uncomplicated: "You can either eat that spinach or sit there until you do." Our duty was to mind, to behave.

So I was dumbfounded one day when I was asked for my opinion about an important matter my folks were considering-whether we should stay where we were in the city or move to the country. All I could muster was, "I don't know." A fortunate answer, it turned out, because Dad wanted to move but Mom wanted to stay.

Both of them were born and raised on the farm. Mom, being anxious to better herself, had gone away to normal school, then taught in town for a time. Thus she acquired a taste for the refinements of the city—indoor plumbing, electric lights, milk delivered in bottles, street cars, next-door neighbors, fire sales and so on. Dad only went through the eighth grade; schooling couldn't teach you to plow a straight furrow. So he favored the country's advantages—room to roam, the sweet smells of harvest, frog gigging, Sunday hardball games, overalls and mack-inaw, buggy races.

His surpassing aspiration had always been a tryout with the

Chicago Cubs. He got offered the tryout but it came when he and Mom were courting in earnest and she wouldn't hear of it. Ballplayers had an unsavory reputation in those days, and a doubtful future. Love triumphed over baseball; they married and took up housekeeping in South Bend, a city in Indiana where a young couple could get ahead.

Even in the good years Dad longed for the farm. When the Depression hit and times turned hard, his longing surged and at every turn for the worse he'd bring up moving to a farm. While we were watching some sandlot game or cleaning out the cistern he'd entice me with the delights of a rural youth: daring leaps from barn loft to hay mow, listening to a hound turn a rabbit, spring dips in the cold creek, the unlocked freedom of woods and fields.

If Mom suspected I was being influenced, she would counter. While I was doing the dishes and she kept finding more that hadn't been used but needed washing, I'd hear the benefits of living in town: friends close by to play with, sidewalks to skate on, penny candy at the corner store, cowboy movies on Saturday afternoons at the Armo.

I straddled the issue until one day I asked Dad, "If we lived on a farm, I could have a dog couldn't I?" "Why sure," he said, "that's the place for a dog, out where he can run and hunt."

I was ready to move. Then one hot afternoon a thin, sickly brown dog wandered up to our house and took refuge under the front porch. I crawled under to see him, in spite of warnings that you should always leave a sick dog alone. Mom let me give him water; I shouldn't feed him because he might belong to somebody and would go home when he got hungry. He didn't; he stayed for days. Each morning when he was still there my hopes grew. He gained strength, moved around the yard but still didn't leave.

Finally, I asked permission to feed him. Mom pondered a bit, then said, "Well, I suppose you can keep him, providing he stays outside. Your father doesn't want dogs in the house."

As far as I knew, moving to the farm never came up again.

That stray dog settled into our lives, eventually gaining in-the-house privileges. He was a "police dog" with a crooked hind leg, alert spirit and uncanny intelligence. He had an insatiable urge to tag along so I named him Tag. When I left for school he had to be shut inside but once he tracked me two miles and up three flights to my high-school homeroom. Most mornings when Mom let him out Tag followed our mailman, Mr. Cruise, to keep him company and protect him from unfriendly canines along the route. At a certain place Mr. Cruise would say, "Go home, Tag. See you tomorrow." Tag would trot home.

He ran the bases with us during ball games, chased us on paths in the snow when we played fox and geese, knew when he was "it." He was a good watch dog, especially offended by drunks who staggered down our street at night.

After my sisters married and moved away and I went off to the service in World War II, Tag centered his attention on my parents, as if to fill the void. It was news of Tag that I looked for in Mom's letters, like how he spent evenings sitting out on the front porch with Dad, hardly flicking an ear when a squirrel came down from the locust tree to eat nuts from Dad's hand. Then, mysteriously, mention of Tag stopped. I was afraid to inquire; I suspected they were sparing me bad news. Only after I returned from overseas did my father take me aside and relate, gently and with unusual feeling, how Tag had grown old and pained with mange and cancer, how Dad had walked him, tagging slowly behind, to the vet and his final merciful rest.

Almost 50 years later I again faced that big decision of whether to move or stay where I was living. I thought about Tag, and how he had made deciding so simple. By now I'd been urbanized, living the apartment life without benefit of yard or trees or birds, much less a dog. I had been laid off from my job. I'd seen it coming; rumor gave warning. I knew I'd survive somehow because it had happened before.

Even so, when my notice came, I suffered the trauma all over again. Decrying the injustice and plotting revenge against somebody, anybody. Updating the resume. Reading the want ads. Filing for unemployment. Realizing the job I'd lost was better than I thought. Exhausting the litany of empty reassurances with fellow victims. Showing up late for work. Eat-drink-and-be-merry farewells.

Then the healing signs of relief: I am rid of that boss. No more meetings or memos. No commuter traffic. My time is my own. I can wear what I want.

Gradually, ultimately, came inspiration: I am free! No employer to satisfy. Divorced, kids on their own, no obligations. Here at last is my chance To Write! Starve in a frigid garret turning out works of great promise that would one day be recognized as literature, posthumously at least.

But the garrets in Washington, D.C., where I'd lived for 14 years were too expensive to starve in. I must move. But where?

Some place cheap, a small town, secluded, with woods and... No, I should be systematic, set up criteria and find a place that meets them.

I worked deductively, from what I didn't like about where I had lived to what I wanted. The data was at hand; in my varied careers I had lived in 14 states, traveled to 42. Wherever my work took me, I imagined what it would be like to live there.

In due time I had my criteria: a place with a sense of community; small town near a big one with cultural events within driving distance; reasonable cost of living; changing seasons; near, but not too near, my kids; an airport nearby; seclusion for writing; nobody living above me or below; a place to jog; a good library; a newspaper worth reading; challenging but cheap golf course; sports teams worth following; outlets for work if I have to resort to honest labor; a place I can be proud to tell others I'm from.

Each factor was weighted from 1 to 10 according to its importance to me. From maps I selected 14 city areas as possible choices, read up on them in the library, sent for information from chambers of commerce, subscribed to their newspapers for a week.

Applying my criteria narrowed the 14 to four, which I visited. That cut the list to two. Closest to my criteria was Madison, Indiana, a picture-postcard old river town of 12,000 inhabitants hidden in a valley on a bend of the Ohio River, 20 miles from any interstate. It is such a small-town prototype that Hollywood producers shoot movies there and magazine editors feature it as down-home quaint. Madison is so generally unspoiled that 113 blocks of its downtown area are listed on the National Registry of Historic Places. Road signs coming into town call it Historic Madison.

It is two towns. An upper "hilltop" tier is standard suburbia, ranchhouse subdivisions clustered behind a multilane franchise corridor of industrial plants, branch banks, discount stores, strip centers with outlets for fast food, gasoline, groceries, hardware, shoes, drugs, video movies, fireworks and other necessities.

A steep, curling drive down the hill on a bluff-sided road with vistas of the valley is a trip back 150 years in time, to a downtown that is a 19th century architectural museum. Along Main Street buildings of diverting variety stand side by side—the spare lines of Federal and Georgian design accentuating the ornate decoration of Italianate and Gothic, Regency and Greek Revival. Tall, slim windows crowned with fretwork and scroll rise stately under garrish overhangs and temple-like entrances, their trim colors both clashing and blending. Church steeples spike into the sky above luxuriant trees.

Residential streets are enhanced by dignified restored mansions and small shotgun houses nondescript but for showy gingerbread. Any town has a spate of handsome houses and exceptional buildings, often spoiled by artless shabby surroundings. In Madison, the display is nearly continuous.

I read my three-days-late Madison paper, took encouragement from the front-page stories about folks and doings that would never make it into a big-city paper. I scoured the classifieds for rentals, sent in a wanted-to-rent ad. Only one answer came, an intriguing one. But ads can be deceiving so another visit to Madison was in order. This time I got on the phone and checked out rentals. One landlord had already rented his apartment but spent an hour chatting, promoting the town. I did drivebys, then got out and walked to get the feel of the surroundings. It was spring now and walking in Madison brought an odd sense of deja vu, from the sidewalks. They were the sidewalks of my youth—blocks of whitish concrete hardened with memories of skating and hopscotch, walks to school, step-on-a-crack-and-break-your-mother's-back, foot slides on icy patches. Familiarity flowed from the street signs, weeds, old houses, overhanging trees.

When I phoned the woman who had answered my ad she invited me to come see the apartment and to have lunch at her house across the street. Mary was as congenial as the golden retrievers who greeted me at the door and as sunny as her porch overlooking the river. She headed a partnership formed to buy an old house nearby, circa 1870, and convert it into apartments.

The house had a tinge of notoriety. Its most recent owner had been controller of a local firm from which he had purloined funds for years to support high living his salary could not. Ultimately he made a stupid mistake, got caught, and was sent to jail. The place was sold to Mary's group to recoup some of his plunder.

My inspection of the apartment convinced me. It was smaller than I was accustomed to, but cozier, had a large kitchen-dining-living room with a huge flagstone fireplace, a second bedroom upstairs with a low, slanted ceiling and window with a view of the river—the struggling writer's garret!

My criteria had not included "a place where I could have a dog," but after I moved to Madison I acquired one, then another, then a third. My daily regimen soon included two or three hours of wanderings with the dogs all over town and into the countryside, in all weathers. Such outings were not only good for my health and theirs, but afforded me time to ruminate, like taking one's thoughts out for a walk. This book is a collection of musings incubated on those jaunts.

It is also a narrative of life with dogs as family and contains all the ingredients of a bestseller:

> Sex—a beagle whose amorous adventures get him tossed in the slammer.
>
> Chases—dog-cat, dog-rabbit, dog-squirrel, dog-dog, cat-dog.
>
> Violence—a pretty German shepherd abused by a skunk.
>
> Conflict—dog walkers versus lawn lovers.
>
> Controversy—sly, sometimes stinging commentaries on the animal behavior of humans and the human behavior of animals.

I wish to acknowledge my support group of First Readers: Mary Clashman, Marykay Gaines, Wanda Hoffman, Katie Meskill and Susan Spaid. They reviewed my drafts and tried to keep me honest, clear and relevant.

Tally Morgan dealt with my digressions, kept me correct, and did what an editor does best—improved the book.

As a literary model, which I couldn't begin to emulate, I followed the essays of E.B. White about moving from New York City and his life as a saltwater farmer in Maine, collected in <u>One Man's Meat</u> (Harper & Row, 1983).

As much as possible I have sought to make my reports on people, places and events truthful. Occasionally I have substituted fictitious names for actual ones. Once in a while I have given my subject matter a fanciful treatment, because a writer is entitled to some entertainment. So the recommended posture for reading this book is with tongue in cheek. That's where mine will be.

AMIGO

# 1 Amigo

A landlady who lets a tenant have a dog is tolerant. One who wants a renter to have a dog is rare. But a landlady who insists you have a dog, and sets about getting you one, is a pearl of great price.

Mary was such a jewel. Soon after I settled into my new apartment in Madison, she began hinting. First: "You really need a dog." Then: "A dog would add a lot to your life." Finally the hard sell: "You could do a lot for some dog who needs a home."

She was not intrusive, but from the first day it was evident she would be no repetition of those absentee urban landlords I never heard from as long as the rent was paid on time. Here I would be more than mere tenant, would be cared about, maybe even cared for. Before I moved in Mary and Georgia, the widow and part owner who occupied the front apartment, had given my empty place a woman's touch—drapes and curtains neatly shaped and a cot, blankets, table and chairs for use until my furniture arrived. Because I couldn't cook, I was often invited to dinner.

That first summer I was drawn into a convivial ritual at Mary's house called "porch time," a quieter, sit-down variation on the happy hour practiced elsewhere. Each weekday evening at 5, Mary holds court on her outside porch overlooking the river. Standing invitations go out in the spring with Mary's vernal greeting cards. She's a single woman in mid-life with few kin; she doesn't do Christmas, she celebrates spring. The rules of porch time, posted on a plaque, decree that festivities shall cease at 6:30, unless conversation is especially spirited, in which case an hour's extension is granted. The drinks are of fine stock and to order, the snacks copious.

Discussions vary as widely as the guests—affairs of state and nation, the weather, world travel and garbage collection, who runs the town and who pretends to, which neighbors are feuding, where to get your car or your teeth fixed, and other valuable intelligence.

Always on duty to greet guests were Smiling Sam and Butterscotch Candy, Mary's plump and gregarious golden retrievers, her house dogs. On her tree farm a few miles out of town were the farm dogs—Frisky, a matronly German shepherd who ran the place, her overgrown silvery son Shadow, and Honey, a doleful-eyed Chihuahua in a beagle body who was one of Mary's welfare cases, found badly injured and brought back to health and a happy home.

Mary is known around town as the "animal lady," an appellation she has not sought but perpetuates because she can't help herself. Morning may find a litter of kittens or a puppy abandoned on her doorstep, dropped by sneaks who salve weak consciences by unburdening their problem on "someone who will give them a good home." Any hour of day or night she may get a call from police or townspeople concerned about some wounded cat, starving horses, or dog chained in the hot sun without water. Madison's animal control officer is one who takes his job description literally and can't be found when an animal needs help, not control. So Mary keeps her car trunk provisioned with blankets, food, water, and first-aid equipment and she has developed a cadre of other caring persons to help out. Before long I was one.

I came to see Mary as the consummate dog person, golden retriever class. Before Sam and Scotch there had been Yo Yo, a prize winner and companion when Mary was an accountant with a big auditing firm in Washington and Indianapolis. Before Yo Yo there was Big Billy, who had won her heart to golden retrievers.

Mary's house is dogproofed—bric-a-brac kept on high shelves, carpets of color close to dog fur, inscribed feeding bowls, dog doors to the fenced-in yard, washable covers on couch and chairs, where snoozing is permitted except when company comes. One chair is a favorite for both Scotch and Sam. When Scotch has occupancy, Sam will slyly approach Mary for a little affection. Seeing scratching being administered, envious Scotch will get down to go for her share, whereupon Sam sneaks over to claim the chair, already well warmed.

Mary's canine family reminded me that a dogless life is a truncated life. Years of travel and no-pet apartments had separated me from the civilizing influence of dogs. My last benefactor had been Penny, a Dalmatian with a black eye acquired when I achieved the status of head of a family of three kids and a house in the suburbs. A dog was needed to complete the picture.

Penny was the only dog I ever bought, $20 as the runt of the litter. She grew to become what my son called "aristocratic," fiercely loyal and protective, with an uncanny capacity to relate differently and equally to each member of the family. She made daily rounds to steal from cat dishes and collect handouts from neighbors who missed her if she didn't come around. Penny was my companion on late-night walks, when I did my profound thinking. She'd go about her private prowlings and all but disappear until we reached a corner, where we met by agreement so I could see us safely across the street for another block of private prowling and profound thinking.

"Well," said Mary in a put-up-or-shut-up tone, "when do you want to go and see Amigo?"

She had picked out the dog for me, matched me and Amigo, a German shepherd at the vet's awaiting proper placement. I hesitated, by habit concerned that my work might involve travel, which Mary dispatched by offering to keep the dog while I was gone. My wariness over the apartment being too small and traffic too near were not worthy of response. Mary sensed that Amigo was a dog I couldn't resist.

She was right. At Dr. Petscher's, Amigo was a sudden black presence moving excitedly from one of us to the other, tail aswish. A magnificent creature! I wasn't prepared for a homeless dog of such beauty. All black except for brown-tan lower legs and white markings on shoulders and throat. Ears perked in the alertness of German shepherds. Moving in grace.

She had been the sole companion of an elderly man who had died on Christmas Day. His relatives didn't want the dog, took her to the vet with instructions to put her to sleep—a full blood, only two years old. Dr. Petscher offered to find her a home.

Mary stood aside while I admired Amigo. No need to put the question: Do you want her? Who wouldn't?

I said I wanted to think it over, knowing all manner of thinking wouldn't change the outcome. For a week or so I did think it over, while shopping for dog dishes, leashes, chow and other canine paraphernalia.

It was a cold day in January when I went to collect her. She came along agreeably enough on the leash and got into the back seat of the car without fuss. But once I drove away she began scrambling from window to window, panting in fright. I talked, trying to calm her. She scurried back and forth, seeking escape. Her breath fogged over the windows and I had to wipe off the windshield to see.

Once home, her anxiety subsided only when she found refuge under the kitchen table. She hovered there, withdrawn against the wall, bewildered.

All my reticence about keeping her was gone. Amigo was not sure, but I was committed.

# 2 The Tie That Bonds

Amigo just laid there in the corner under the kitchen table for hours, day and night. Hunched down on her belly, head on her paws, ears laid back. She followed me with her eyes—furtive, suspicious. If I approached, she lifted her head as if bracing to defend herself.

"It's all right, girl," I'd say and stroke her lustrous black fur, scratch behind her ears. She tolerated this but when I quit she seemed relieved. She had been so friendly at the vet's, now she was leery of me.

I put food and water in bowls on the floor across the room but they went untouched. I moved the bowls over under the table beside her; she ignored them. She did lie on the rug I put down for her, as if it were part of her refuge. When in the house, she never moved from her tiny corner of security.

Only outside did she show any spirit. If I approached her with the leash, she responded; a walk must have meant a chance at freedom. She'd follow along sullenly, showing interest only in the scent markings on trees and bushes, a cat hiding under a car or barking by other dogs. Once back home, she fled to her place under the table.

After a few days her food showed nibble marks where she had tried it. I gave her milk, which she was too anxious to keep down.

She never barked, ever. Occasionally at night I would hear her flop down, changing positions. I never heard her scratch. Amigo was giving me the silent treatment.

We were in the bonding period, which the vet had said would take about 60 days. I was to keep her close; owner and pet need time to adjust to each other.

An organization in California that matches and trains dogs and people with disabilities has a seven-day "leash-up" period when human and animal are literally leashed together all day and all night—eating, sleeping, dressing, working, traveling, doing everything (yes, everything) within five feet of each other. It's make or break; the forced intimacy may reveal quickly that the two don't fit. If the bind-bond takes, the two are off to a wondrous partnership.

Amigo was no pliant puppy. She was two years old, fully grown and imprinted with past loyalties and learnings unknown to me. I was patient but yearned for her acceptance. As I worked alone upstairs at night, I was keen to the presence of a dog in the house and sometimes found myself saying her name, "Amigo...Amigo." A minor mistranslation of the Spanish—female "friend" would be Amiga—but a pleasing sound and I wanted its meaning to be true.

We took walks two, three or more times every day, in every weather. The bracing cold stimulated and cheered us. We ventured into 14-below numbness one still night, mutually agreed to abbreviate our outing and raced home to the warm relief of the house.

Occasionally at day's end after we had shared the brisk outdoors and I sat at my desk attempting to work I'd feel a sad separation from her, asleep downstairs under the kitchen table. Then I'd rouse her for another walk.

Soon we knew the turf and bark of every canine guardian along our way. Our approach set off the territorial alarm system when the duty dog challenged us, alerting another down the block who signaled the next, until the entire security force was on the lookout for approaching intruders.

I bought a longer leash to gave Amigo greater range. By looping the end around one hand and playing it out as needed through the other, I managed both freedom and control. Training was not my purpose in these excursions, so I let her lead. I took charge of strategy (which direction to go, how far, and so on) and she decided tactics (where to stop for investigation and how long).

As the weather moderated and more people were about, Amigo drew the admiring comment, "Pretty dog," repeated with monotonous predictability. I was proud strolling with such a raven beauty.

Amigo doesn't have the classic confirmation of the German shepherd —deep, muscular chest and long, low-slung hindquarters. She's almost svelte, with the slight-strong legs of a dancer, a sable silhouette flowing from pricked-up ears to her tall tapered tail, a creature of grace.

She has wiry strength, I learned when some bold cat would dart across our path and Amigo lunged, yanking the leash taut and pulling me after her. She took intense interest in Misty, the next-door cat, who was equally interested in Amigo. When Misty walked by outside, curious and teasing, Amigo dashed to the French doors, which give a dog's-eye view of the yard, and whimpered in frustration. I was glad for such vitality, a sign she was emerging from her malaise.

Amigo's reaction to kids was puzzling. She was wary when we approached them and cowered close to me when they surrounded us, accepting their pats uncomfortably. If we came upon a playground of boys shooting baskets, she crouched and pulled back in panic. Fear seized her whenever we came within earshot of a bouncing ball or the shrill shouts of children.

If a passing car backfired, I had to hold firmly to keep her from running wild. She was spooked, bad memories were working in her. Those frightening episodes may have driven her closer to me. I gave in to her need to flee from what menaced her, then drew her to a stop and talked to her, knelt down, tried to calm and reassure her. Back home, when she'd regained her security corner, she would look up at me, still shaken, as if grateful to be home with me. Once or twice when I told her good night as I left her to go to bed, she wagged her tail, ever so slightly.

Our outings must have been new adventures for Amigo. Her life before had been limited to staying home all day while her owner worked, then a walk in a nearby cemetery. We expanded our explorations to new parts of town.

Alleys became our preferred route; they were more intriguing and informative. People encountered in front, sitting on the porch or watering a well-kept lawn, were stiffer, their greetings grudging. Here, too, was the No-Pee Patrol: "Don't you let that dog do anything in my yard."

Life is not so restricted out back. Pretensions seem to fall away with the exposure of unkempt sheds and littered garages, trash, gardens gone to weeds, intimate apparel on clotheslines. Householders come upon in the act of cleaning up some mess are informal, open to talk. As conversation moves from weather or the task at hand I am regularly asked, "Are you from Madison?" I came to recognize this was not casual conversation but social reconnaissance, the small-town equivalent of "Halt! Who goes there?" The answer identifies one as friend or foe.

Partially to escape such scrutiny we took to open country for our daytime jaunts and walked the streets at night when residents had gone indoors. Late night was our favorite time, when vans and pickups were parked and people had gone to bed. A strange and wonderful silence settled on the streets. Nature came forth: cats on the prowl, dogs barking more in greeting than warning, a rabbit or possum scampering across an alley, crickets in concert and birds murmuring in the trees. You could hear your footsteps crunching in leaves or snow.

One clear frigid night we sighted the dark figure of a woman emerging from an alley. She made for us, tottering, her coat carelessly open to the cold. The smell of booze preceded her and her greeting was slurred. Out of courtesy we stopped and soon were drawn into the loquacious soliloquy of the lonely drunk. She had a dog, too, but not much of one. She had a husband; he was not much either. She lived nearby, I couldn't make out where. She had questions but hardly heard my answers.

Amigo tugged at the leash to get going. I began my parting comments and suddenly the woman moved forward and kissed me, soundly, right on the lips!

I was stunned. A safe distance away, I reconnoitered. This must be a real friendly town.

Amigo welcomed her snug, warm corner after our foray in the cold. As I snuggled under the blankets I heard the sound of something moving in the dark. It was Amigo, walking around in my bedroom. I waited and listened. I heard her flop down in a corner near my bed. Until now she had never slept anywhere but under the kitchen table. I switched on the night-table lamp to check. She never moved, only opened her eyes for a moment and then closed them, settled for sleep.

I turned off the light and lay in the dark, quietly thrilled.

# 3 Training by the Book

Research shows that in any given year about 70 per cent of adults undertake a learning project of their own. Some circumstance—baby on the way, new hobby, travel, house redecorating, weight problem, new apparatus—stimulates them to read, take classes, bone up on the subject. Once I was engaged to marry a woman like that. She studied up on our impending union so thoroughly, from a book entitled <u>Second Wife</u>, that she called off the engagement.

I'm a bit that way, too, although it didn't occur to me to research second marriages until I got dumped. Now I faced learning to live with another female, with whom I'd already set up housekeeping. This time I would not fail. Maybe it would be easier with canines. I frequented the library and bookstores, read dog periodicals, sent off for stuff and assembled a rather impressive bibliography on the care and training of dogs—a subject covered more extensively than second marriages.

I figured Amigo was lucky. For decades I'd been training adults all over the country on all kinds of subjects. I'd written books on training. A dog couldn't be any tougher than some humans I'd encountered.

But in no time I came down with a bad case of mental bloat. Authors tended to presume that theirs was the only definitive book on the subject so the treatment was encyclopedic, more than I cared to know but not necessarily what I needed to know. Much on training the new puppy but precious little about a mature dog. In-depth information on every exotic affliction known to the species but hardly anything on how to keep an older dog healthy.

Here, too, was an enigma that permeates human instruction—the anybody-can-train syndrome. It is widely believed that training requires no special skills or preparation. Anyone who knows something about something can pontificate on it. A degree in veterinary medicine can be stretched to cover the training of animals. Breeders, handlers, anybody around animals can declare themselves expert and bring out a book or video.

As usual, the experts disagreed, primarily on methods. Most animal trainers are of the positive-reinforcement school, which rewards desired performance with an encouraging word or gesture. Goofs are ignored or met with mild scolding or a harmless slap. A few of the spare-the-rod school believe in "correction" by shock, delivered with force or bizarre electrical contrivances, claiming "results" justify such methods.

The trainer/writer can be as authoritarian as a schoolmarm and direct a hapless dog owner to follow certain procedures which admit no differences in dogs and/or owners. "Obedience training" is the common prerequisite for a canine's admission to the human world, intended to turn a tumble of exuberant energy into a model of submission. An advanced form is for "working breeds" who exhibit their obedience skills to win ribbons, cups and the ego satisfaction of their handlers. These show animals are not to be confused with working dogs who do honest labor— sheep herders, guide dogs, helpers of the handicapped, drug sniffers, rescue dogs.

Even at the elementary level, obedience training is laden with overkill. Insisting that a pooch walk only on the left and a half pace behind the owner and come to heel at every corner does not seem essential to keeping the owner s household happy and intact or prevent her from being hurt, sued or arrested.

Some advice on care seemed equally excessive. Brushing the rascal every single day, clipping his toenails once a week, even brushing his teeth, for god's sake. That's fine for gussied-up show-off dogs, but hardly appropriate for the plain old ordinary owner with a plain old ordinary mutt—and a life beyond dogdom to live.

A few authors drew a useful distinction between the "old school" and "new school" in dog training. The evolution is in human regard for the animal, from the perception of a raw beast to be tamed by frequent punishment to regard for the dog as a creature of individuality capable of responding in a partnership of human and animal. From both inclination and experience, I signed on with the new school.

My exploration of canine education brought me out believing that what I needed was there, somewhere, buried in all that I didn't need. To winnow out the useable, I fell back on the needs-assessment process used in adult ed, ingraciously termed "front-end analysis." The job to be performed is examined for the knowledge, skills and attitude required. Then the trainee's a priori possession of the requirements is assessed. The difference between what is needed and what is known is what must be learned.

What did Amigo need to perform her job? To come when I call her. To stay close by. To stop when danger threatens. To cease and desist from misbehavior. To quit barking when requested.

My list of job requirements was surprisingly short. I wasn't out to teach her cute tricks or have her bring in the newspaper or attack an intruder. I just wanted a reasonably well behaved dog.

Assessing her present behavior didn't add much to be learned. She was already housebroken, seldom barked and not unnecessarily. She never got up on the furniture or chewed on things or got in the way. She did pester me to go out, which was due partly to her past history of confinement and partly to our mutual enjoyment of walks.

The behavior that bothered me most was her fear, even terror brought on when approaching kids playing basketball or by the sharp sudden sounds of a car backfiring or a firecracker going off. Too deeply instilled to be reached by obedience training.

Having determined the learning objectives for Amigo, I consulted my sources and chose a simple program for her: Sit-Heel-Come-Stay-Down. I was less certain I could meet the requirements for me: Firmness tempered with kindness. Strict but gentle. Consistency and patience. Control and discipline. So what? I raised three kids with less and they turned out fine.

I simply ignored the admonitions with macho appeal: the dog must be mastered, must never be the winner in confrontations. Otherwise, I would train by the book. Short sessions, ten minutes three times a day with no distractions. I set up a schedule. Don't start a new lesson until the old one is learned. Begin with an easy lesson: <u>Sit</u> seemed like a good place to start.

I called her to me in the center of the distraction-free living room and announced my objective for the session; that's the way we do it in people training. Giving the crisp command "Sit!" I pulled her head up by the leash in one hand and pushed her hind end down with the other. She resisted momentarily, then got the idea and sat down. "Good girl!"

The book called for repetition. The second time, as soon as I pushed on her rear quarters, she sat right down. The third time, she sat down as soon as I touched her, then swished her tail across the floor as if this was fun. "Show her you won't tolerate any fooling around," saith the book. "German shepherds will try to get away with as much as you let them." So I lectured her sternly about the importance of taking this seriously.

Next try, she resisted sitting, until I almost had to shove her to the floor. Well, that was enough for one lesson, anyway.

We took a long walk to restore our friendly relations, during which she encountered a kitten in a bush. Amigo poked her nose at the tiny thing in a curious, friendly greeting and was met with an arched-spine hiss and snarl that sent Amigo backing out in surprise and disappointment. Fine thing, I told her, intimidated by a kitty one-tenth your size.

Next lesson, Amigo did beautifully, so well that I dropped the pull-push routine and merely commanded "Sit" and she sat. We repeated the exercise several times, as the book instructed. Right every time, so I lavished her with the prescribed praise. In the joy of the moment she leaped up on me.

I knew that was a no-no. Back to the book, which offered the correction: put your knee in her chest and push so she falls down. During the next session when we were doing a review of Sit, she again responded to my positive reinforcement by jumping up on me. I kneed and pushed; she sidestepped adroitly and I did the falling down.

She graduated from one command to the next rather quickly, as long as we stuck with one command per lesson. Mixing Stay and Come was confusing; she clearly preferred Come. Down was difficult; the instruction to push her down on command and pull her legs out from under her if necessary was more like wrestling than training. Maybe it was my fault; I didn't seem to get the "downward inflection" in the order "Dooowwwwnnn" that was called for.

I dispensed with Heel. The notion that she must forever walk in back of me, at my left heel, and never poke her nose a smidgen in front was contrary to the roaming freedom she'd had on our walks and smacked of a ritual intended to puff up the superiority of the Master.

Conscientious as I was, and despite Amigo's valiant endeavor to figure out just what the hell I wanted, something untoward crept into the training. It was a confrontation of sorts; *me* versus *her*. Our walks became a battle of wits, even without any use of commands. She was contentious about going her way, or staying when I wanted to move on; I was testy about her rebellion. Tug and pull, scold and sulk. Soon we were adversaries instead of friends.

All the grim admonitions of the book came down on me: You have to be master. Teach her respect. She must learn to obey. My male conditioning asserted itself: You must dominate. What kind of a man are you, anyway?

It took some heavy rationalization to decide I didn't want to dominate for the sake of dominating and I didn't get Amigo just to conquer her. Besides, even if she learned every command, I couldn't see that Sit-Heel-Come-Stay-Down would make our life together more than a continuing contest.

I abandoned the lessons. What a trainer I turned out to be. I couldn't even train a dog.

# 4 Native or Not?

If I have been asked "Are you from Madison?" once, I've been asked umpteen dozen times. The question comes up early in polite conversation with someone of residential seniority, like a cop who has stopped you offering a courteous greeting, then asking to see your driver's license.

If my reply, "No, I'm not," brings a sidewise glance of suspicion I know I've engaged a proctor of the Ancient and Protective Order of Nativeborns. During the casual interrogation that follows I will be covertly classified as to the status of citizenship I may henceforth enjoy.

This minding of a small town's social borders is to protect against outsiders who might move in and take over. If such invaders cannot be fended off at least they can be labeled and watched.

The Order is informal but united in purpose. Members recognize each other by code phrases having to do with the past, like what was located where the K-Mart is now or meeting relatives from Kokomo when Greyhound buses used to stop here. I've witnessed the cross-questioning of Order members heretofore unknown to each other and observed their relieved recognition from the exchange of correct answers, like tourists coming upon someone from back home while visiting Kuala Lumpur.

The instantly acceptable answer to the test question is, "Oh yes, I was born in Madison, have lived here all my life." This classifies the respondent as Citizen First Class. (An exemption is granted, out of patriotic duty, for time spent living away from town in military service.)

Certain privileges accrue only to citizens of the first rank. Your name, along with your forebears, can appear in the genealogy column of the local paper. You may attend the Old Settlers Picnic. Above all, you are eligible to run for public office with a fair certainty of election if running against a candidate of lesser rank, that is, an *outsider*.

Viable candidates run on a platform declaring that they were born, reared and have lived continuously in the city or county along with their 2.7 children, parents and grandparents and have never been contaminated by outside ideas or influence. Some may advertise themselves as Honest, Efficient and Experienced, but this is not essential. The only contested elections are between fellow members of the Order; in one such race a lifelong resident exposed as having spent a year in Chicago tending bar in a brothel was soundly defeated. It was the year in absentia that did him in.

If one fails the born-here question, the next is: "How long have you lived here?" An exact date of origin must be supplied because every city has a benchmark against which it measures those who are not native, but may qualify for Citizen Second Class. The cutoff dates are invariably the occasion of some cataclysmic event. For communities up and down the Ohio River, the 1937 Flood separates Second Class Citizens (B.F., or Before the Flood) from interlopers. The demarcation can change, however, and indeed for Madison and ravaged places nearby the 1974 Tornado became the new time-certain event.

If you lived here *before* the 1974 Tornado you are classified Citizen Second Class (B.T.) with secondary rights and privileges. These are ill defined; it requires some experimentation to find out what one can get away with. In view of this, the system may withhold rights or at least the privilege of social acceptance until one has been proven not to be an outside agitator. If a Second Class Citizen becomes overactive—e.g., suggesting that change of any sort be undertaken—then the stigma of the New Here Class attaches, which is only a touch above Tourist Class and marks its members as Not To Be Taken Seriously.

Such fuzzy strictures are particularly confining to the sizeable number of rather affluent persons who decide to retire to Madison, perhaps purchase and restore a neglected but historic house. Most learn to live quietly and earn limited status by their acquiescence. One retired minister who moved here from another place, a social gospeler, set about becoming active in long-undisturbed but needful matters, even to the point of writing letters to the editor advocating improvements. His name became anathema, his efforts came to naught, and he soon passed into ignominy.

Any town worth a tourist's dollar has rummaged through its past for whatever might approximate a claim to fame. Sometimes the vein of history runs so shallow that a bit of creative exaggeration is necessary—the George-Washington-slept-here treatment. A near-skirmish in the Civil War will do; any discovery or first or oldest, say the invention of corn flakes or coat hangers, first use of wind socks or oldest jail in a freestanding building in the state. Celebrities are exploitable, no matter how brief their residence or fame. Even a hoax is permissible, if it is entertaining and presented as believable.

Madison qualifies. Jenny Lind, the Swedish Nightingale made famous and rich by P.T. Barnum, once sang in Madison at a slaughterhouse later called the Jenny Lind Pork House. She is now memorialized by a bed and breakfast and a craft shop that sells buttons.

Morgan's Raiders ravaged through Southern Indiana in 1863; Madison answered the call to arms, hastily formed militia companies of 60 self-armed citizens, elected officers, shut down business, set to drilling and declared themselves "ready to crush out the enemies of our peerless Union (5,000 mounted men with artillery), we are tranquil but fearless, energetic and resolute. Hurrah for us." Alas, Morgan bypassed Madison. Only a few obscure markers in villages out in the county recall where his outriders galloped through.

Tradition has it, a way of saying it probably isn't true but we wish it were, that one of the town's mansions was built with a loan secured by the unseen contents of a trunk deposited with a bank. When the borrower disappeared and wasn't heard from, the bank opened the trunk to find worthless paper.

Madison hardly needs such folderal. Its past is rich and illustrious; considerably moreso, in fact, than its present.

In the late 1700's landseekers streaming westward down the Ohio River put in at the cluster of lean-tos and log cabins a few hours below Cincinnati. From there they could strike north over the Michigan Road hacked out of an Indian trail that led to Lake Michigan.

Some migrators settled in Madison, enough to cause a small population explosion. The settlement grew from 954 inhabitants to 1,752 in a decade, making it the largest and wealthiest in the state then occupied predominately by Indians.

Outfitting travelers bound for the Northwest Territory was the town's first business. But its providential location on the river opened commerce with suppliers and markets upriver in Wheeling, Pittsburgh and Cincinnati and downriver as far as New Orleans. The frontier town expanded, industrialized, became a hub for riverboat traffic.

Progress for the next 50 years was led by "men of foresight and daring" with an eye for trade. John Paul, considered the town's founder, was a shrewd land speculator, bought 691 acres which he cut up into lots offered for sale to "Mechanics of all descriptions, Merchants and Gentlemen of Professorial character, DOCTORS only excepted." Most of the city fathers were merchants.

They took on laying a plank road over the Indian trail to the north, as much to help farmers move their hogs to market as to ease the way of migrants. They tackled a 10-year project of building a railroad to Indianapolis, carving a narrow trackbed through the limestone hills north of town up the steepest rail incline in the world.

To the shops and mills turning out everything from ironworks and furniture to buttons and castor oil, entrepreneurs added the processing of farm products—so much pork the town challenged Cincinnati's claim to be "Porkopolis." So many wild hogs roamed at will a hog pound had to be built.

Culture was not neglected. Madison established the first public library in the territory. The wealthy elite erected elegant mansions and ornate business establishments that made the town a mecca for architects and historians for years to come.

What a robust, hard-working, hard-drinking, future-building time that era must have been. Residents waded the swampy streets, dodged wild hogs, drunks (100 saloons) and disorderly citizens, gasped on smoke and soot that made the town dirtier by the year, stopped to watch iron fronting being applied to a mercantile house, set their watches by the peel of the bell in the railroad station tower.

Editors took such passionate editorial positions on politics and commerce that they were challenged to duels by some who disagreed just as fiercely. Michael Christian Garber, who bought and made the newspaper that survives today, wrote with a "pen tinged with fire" against slavery in a town that was more Southern in sentiment than Yankee and challenged the corrupt political boss of the state. Waylaid one day outside the newspaper office by one of the boss's henchmen, he was stabbed three times in the chest with a chisel, nearly dying for his gutsy stands.

A painter whose works today are shown with pride by long-time residents once sold many of them for a bottle of booze.

Even in its era of growth, Madison was beset by forces beyond control—economic depressions, epidemics, fires—fires so frequent and devastating that at one time frame and log buildings were banned.

Then mysteriously, imperceptibly, the bottom fell out. Growth ceased. The pork trade fell by half. River traffic was curtailed, water routes too unreliable in winter when the Ohio froze over. The railroad north never pushed beyond Indianapolis because competing lines found flatter, easier routes. Burgeoning cities of the Midwest that prospered from their own fortunate circumstances robbed Madison of trade. Overextended developers went bankrupt. The moneyed men's failure to lower rates to build affordable housing sent carpenters, bricklayers and artisans looking elsewhere so construction stopped. Hemmed in by its hills with no where to expand, the town's trade area shrunk. Its image as a sinking ship deepened the stagnation.

For almost a century Madison was "the town that time forgot" as one writer termed it or as another said, "Madison just stayed Madison."

The town's rise and fall over time has left it ambivalently stranded between the past and the future. Once the hub of rail, river and overland transport, today it is without public transit of any sort, 20 miles removed from any interstate highway. For some, this isolation is an asset. Well-to-do folk who've had enough of the hectic Big City look on Madison as a refuge and retirement haven. So many have bought up old houses to restore that the stock is limited and prices at a premium.

The annual Big Event for outside exposure is the Madison Regatta, which draws the rooster-tailed hydroplanes for races on the river and a week of festivities each Fourth of July. Just as Louisville residents decry their spring invasion of outsiders even as they make plans for a big Kentucky Derby party and

Indianapolis householders leave town during the Indy 500 and rent out their houses for enough to finance their vacations, Madisonians sniff about the riffraff that the Regatta brings in, but invite family and friends down for the races. And the prediction that "this is probably the last year for the Regatta" comes up as perennially as tulips.

Long gone are the 100 saloons and stumbled-over drunks of the Golden Era. Modern Madison sustains enough downtown watering holes to slake the Saturday-night thirst of imbibers from miles around. But the town has turned churchy so the higher class of people do their drinking at their lodges or slip off to Cincinnati or Louisville to carouse.

Madison may be no more unable to decide whether to go back, stay the same, or go forward than other communities, but here the cause is historic.

Out on the west edge of town on a small knoll above the river's edge sits a tiny crude shack, the domicile of a redoubtable squatter by the name of Mr. Brown. He's a gaunt elderly gentleman of fine manners with a cheerful greeting for me unless he fears Amigo might pester his chickens, who wander and scratch all about the place. Wheelless bicycle frames are the only identifiable items in the trash that litters the hill. Sometimes smoke rises from a fire pit beside the chicken coop.

He does some bike repairing but his real calling is jackleg preacher, undenominated, anointed to speak fervently for the Lord to any who will listen. God speaks to him in doubtfree words that he writes down in a thick looseleaf book.

Mr. Brown has lived in the shack on the hill, undisturbed, rentfree, for as long as anyone I've asked has known, accepted as a harmless, even picturesque eccentric.

Mr. Brown is my inspiration. I wasn't born here and I arrived after the Tornado, but maybe I can gain acceptance as an eccentric, Colorful Character Class.

# 5 Unleashed

Glory be. On a shiny morning like this, how easy for man and dog out for a run to be lifted into that state of harmony where all's right with the world. The day encourages, soft sun glances off the swells and eddies of the ever-constant, ever-changing river, a mariner's wind gusting. The hills of the opposite shore lie bumpy under a green comforter, ignoring bird calls.

At this hour, humanity is off elsewhere in pursuit of commerce and we are left alone.

We prowl the riverbank, Amigo and I, wading into deep brush, treading uncertainly on rocks, stepping over gnarled tree roots, ducking under branches. The going is easier for her; she breaks a hard-to-follow trail so I pick a parallel route. We are in search of small discoveries: a dead catfish is worth a sniff, the swish and plop of a muskrat rushing for water alerts us, overhead a bird sings with that sound that reminds me of the telephone ringing.

We are on the border between man and nature, where the mix is spoiling: beer cans beside a shucked snakeskin, pale rippled shells scattered near a plastic milk jug, mole ruts burrowed under a discarded truck tire. You have to go out far to escape the detritus of civilization.

We wander far, directed by the river, watchful of footing more than time, keen to the scent of a fresh-cut field and the quaking of aspen in a bog where beaver sometimes cruise. Turning back, we follow a fresh track through meadows of purple thistle and Queen Anne's lace bobbing, touching off the bark of an envious dog.

Our return to the populated, paved and close-cut flood plain of town is announced by the rumble of traffic on the bridge above. Amigo lopes ahead to flush a flock of pigeons which takes off from the shore in unison, wheels up, out and down river to alight again at a secure distance. The deed thrills Amigo, coming back tail-tall and head up to share her excitement. She mouths my hand in the careful hold of the love bite. I find a long stick that she immediately grasps in her mouth to tug from me while I pull back on the other end. It is our daily game; if I don't start it, she will find a stick, sometimes too big to handle, to signal her desire to play.

She has become her name, <u>Amigo</u>, my friend. Out here, beyond the constraints of the established order and with the leash in my pocket, we are free from each other, but closer in spirit than if attached. Perhaps the absence of verbal communication opens man and animal to a deeper, surer connection of heart and thought. I share her sudden curiosity at a thrashing in the undergrowth, the furiosity of her chase after a rabbit—me shouting "There he goes! There he goes!"—and her disappointment when it disappears. She senses me struggling up a muddy creek bank and comes back to inquire in a show of concern.

We have become inseparable. I take her everywhere. In the car she has claimed her place in the back seat by the rightside window, head poked out in the wind no matter how cold, rendering the heater useless. We venture into establishments, are accepted quizically in some, are evicted from others, which I boycott: love me; love my dog. Except for the library, that repository of all manner of animal stories, still clinging to a no-pet policy which I observe but will not forgive.

She dozes contentedly on the floor of the barber shop while I get my hair cut, prefers to watch in a corner of the garage when Buck or Don service the car, after one scary try at riding in her seat to the top of the hoist.

She travels well, observes the passing scene until we hit the interstate, which bores her, then curls up on the seat and goes to sleep. Like any three-year-old, she lets me know when she has to go, and we eschew those tiny dogs-must-do-it-here plots at rest stops for the fine fields and interesting woods to be found out behind.

I use the leash only on our walks around town. On many nights now, we are joined by a rugged little beagle who comes from somewhere around a big restored 1890s house on Main Street. He's a friendly cuss with a torn ear and no collar who takes to Amigo as she does to him. He follows around and about for blocks, escorts us home, then disappears.

When first I tried Amigo "off lead" it was in the security of open country. She went wild with freedom. Once loose, she'd dash off for great distances, occasionally beyond my sight or call. It was frightening, for me and her. When I recovered her, I avoided remonstrances, patted and soothed and reassured her. Then I'd walk quietly with her, my hand rubbing her neck, hooked on the leash only when she was content in my company. I didn't want restraint to become punishment.

A day or two on lead, even on the longest runs, seemed to convey the message: stick around. When I gave her new tastes of freedom, her bolts were not as furious and her test runs got shorter and shorter. She loved the exhilaration of being turned loose, like an adolescent allowed to stay out after midnight, but that initial rush of on-her-ownness paled, as the teenager sometimes comes home before curfew.

To reenforce the idea of home base, I tethered Amigo in the yard on one of those chains staked into the ground. Georgia's cat put an end to that. Misty had that cat mix of fear and fascination with Amigo. She'd venture to the edge of her porch, peer out to see if Amigo was around and if so, sprint quickly-back-inside through the door Georgia had left ajar.

Misty soon learned that Amigo was confined and gauged the range of her tether. In an outrageous display of provocation Misty would slither by, just out of reach. Every time she got the chance, driving Amigo berserk.

One morning Misty opted for a dash right through the danger zone. She waited until Amigo was not looking, then darted past a few feet from her tease victim. Amigo was not napping and gave chase immediately—right to the end of the chain, which jerked and spilled Amigo tail over teacups—and snapped in two. No more chaining of Amigo in the yard.

In mild weather I left the French door to the yard open, allowing Amigo to go in and out. I checked on her frequently and usually found her dozing in the grass. Sometimes she'd be gone and I worried, but I'd wait for a time because I wanted her to come back on her own.

Such liberty may have been a mistake. She took such occasions to explore her environs and I heard about it—or overhead about it. A woman down the block complained audibly to a neighbor across the street as I passed by, "He lets that dog run all over the neighborhood." The looks I got when we walked properly down the sidewalk, Amigo closely leashed, were not neighborly. My nods of greeting were not returned.

One day I answered a hard rap at the door to find a frail but formidably outfitted police officer. Was that black dog mine? he wanted to know. He had received complaints of that dog running loose. Did I not know, he asked sternly, that I had to keep that dog either tied up or fenced in or on a leash at all times?

It occurred to me to counter that this was not precisely what the ordinance required but I thought better of it. With the magnanimity of one sparing my life, he said he would let me off with a warning, then carefully repeated his admonition.

A Sunday forenoon a few weeks later Amigo and I were emerging from the ravine below the President Madison Motel, which sits high on a terraced hill overlooking the river, when a police cruiser prowled up an unused road to the motel. It was the last cop I wanted to see.

He pulled up beside me and I called Amigo, following a few feet away, to my side. He opened the car door but remained inside.

"I thought I told you to keep that dog on a leash."

I decided to contend. "This is private property," I began, "and Ray who owns the hotel doesn't care. His kids come out and pet the dog." That slowed him but didn't stop him. "But I warned you," he countered and then repeated his earlier admonition.

I was prepared; I had checked on the "leash law," recently adopted in Madison and patterned after model legislation in effect elsewhere.

"As I understand it," I opened my argument, "the word 'leash' doesn't appear anywhere in the ordinance. The law only says that the dog must be under restraint when it is out."

I paused for effect. "And restraint is defined legally as within voice command of the owner. That's the rule all over the country. There's nothing said about a leash."

He didn't respond; I had him. Foolishly, I inquired, "Have you ever read the ordinance?"

He picked up his portable radio unit and called in. "Do we have a copy of that leash law around?" I heard him ask the dispatcher. We both waited. Amigo gave me a let's-go look.

For five minutes, nothing, then he began writing in his citation book.

"You just go in and see the judge. He'll decide."

The cop's cop-out. He handed me the ticket and drove off without a word. I had made my case, but lost.

My name in the Arrests and Citations listing, most-read column in the local newspaper, added to my notoriety in the neighborhood.

At the appointed hour I appeared at the Courthouse, where the gravity of my summons was lost on those present, preoccupied with important paperwork and chit-chat. Court was not in session and a secretary finally steered me to the office of the county judge. After a nervous wait, I was invited into the rather ordinary chambers of Judge Hoying, a congenial gent who preferred talking of the weather to hearing my case.

"Well, what brings you to visit us?" he asked finally. I proffered my citation and launched into my defense, the whole nine yards.

The judge listened carefully, then picked up the phone and called the police station, asked for the arresting officer. "Well, have him call me," he said, hung up, and inquired if I was a native of Madison, how long I had lived here. The phone rang. The judge listened to the officer's report, asked some pertinent questions, then sluffed it all off as no big deal. Not until I heard myself being invited to drop in again any time did I realize the charge had been dropped. Right had prevailed! I pictured Justice Fred W. Hoying in the flowing robes of the U.S. Supreme Court.

# 6 Reports from the Real World

One of the cultural advantages of a small town is the opportunity to read country correspondence, those weekly write-ups in the paper concerning the state of affairs out at Cross Plains, Saluda, Big Doe Run, Rikers Ridge and such places. For instance:

> Becky Reed has had surgery which consists of gallbladder surgery and some repairs or changes on her esophagus. She had been getting choked easily so hopefully she will soon be able to eat. Monday she was on broth.

You don't get news like that in big city papers. They don't cover things in depth, like:

> Bob and Cindy Quick of Madison spent Saturday forenoon with Don and Doris Dixon. Cindy came to work. She cleaned and polished all of Doris's cabinets.

That brand of journalism is practiced mostly by weeklies. Small town dailies tend to fill their pages with stuff off the press wire and boilerplate features because they figure it costs too much to hire reporters, so people scattered all over the nation subscribe to weeklies back home to get the real news, such as:

> Ronnie Reed had the misfortune to cut two of his toes through his shoe with a weed-eater that had a blade attached to it. Hope Ronnie is doing better and on the mend.

These investigative reports are done by correspondents,

mostly women, who are part busybody, part gossip, all caring, all knowing, like a village grandmother. They are the social glue that holds a community together. Usually, they get paid at space rates, so much a column inch, and not much.

> If you have news for the week of November 29th I will need it by Sunday, the 28th, as I plan to attend income tax school November 29th and 30th at Seymour.

They are women of unashamed piety and not above delivering an editorial sermon:

> Morbus Sabbaticus, or Sunday Sickness, is a disease peculiar to church members. The attack comes suddenly on Sundays. No symptoms are felt on Saturday night. The patient sleeps well, awakens feeling well and eats a hearty breakfast. But about church time the attack comes on and continues until services are over for the morning. Then the patient usually feels better by noon and is able to function normally the rest of the day. A vital faith is the only antidote. No remedy is known for it except repentance and prayer.

They minister to the sick and well by apprising us of who is stricken, reminding us to remember them with our cards and visits and prayers. And they are not intimidated by the medical establishment:

> I just talked to Myrtle Whitham. She's still at Rita's but is doing okay. She went into the hospital for surgery on Monday. They sent her home Tuesday. I think that's too fast but they didn't ask me.

Folk are not forgotten the minute they leave the hospital. We get updates.

> Lucy Brown is about the same except she is being fed a small amount of food by mouth occasionally.

When I was fresh from journalism school, I applied for a job with The Milwaukee Journal, one of the best. I had the gall to question the editor about the paper's practice of covering activities of every social or civic group and printing the names, in agate, of everybody who attended the meeting.

"Names make news," said the editor. "This newspaper's reputation was built on printing names."

Most people used to get their names in the paper only four times in their lives—when they were born, graduated, got married, and died. The rule today should be upgraded to include divorced, sued and arrested, in small type.

Country correspondence happily ignores such rules.

> Rachelle Vest celebrated her first birthday Saturday afternoon, Nov. 13 at one of the Bedford Christian Church's Sunday school rooms with cake and ice cream. She had a whole chocolate cake to herself and loved every minute of it. Those present to help in the celebration were her mother and father, Terry and Regina Vest, Cecil, Rhonda, Rebecca and Rachel Skaggs, Dustin and Devine Williams, Nanna Williams, Mamma and Pappa Vest, Wayne, Michelle, Jessica and Jason Vest, Jerri Cutter, Ashley and Allison Tingle, Christine Lake and Elizabeth, Linda Kirtman, Bob and Kathy Vest of Smithfield. Many happy birthdays in the future, Rachelle.

Getting the names and spelling them right is a test for any journalist but for the country correspondent, it's half the job. Every birthday, wedding, and item beginning "Supper guests of Mr. and Mrs. Cecil Level Saturday evening were..." or "Recent callers were..." is followed by the guest list, except when secret pals are involved, of course.

We are informed not only of who was there but that they had chicken and dressing and cherry, raspberry and peach jelly, all homemade, and if they dined out at the Texas Road House, the Homestead or Long John Silver's, where they went shopping and what for, and presents given like "a handcrafted basket with lace, bows and pretty trim."

Now where on television could you get details like that? Not from the pretty people who read the news, weather and sports, banter in happy talk amongst themselves, then gush about how much they <u>care</u>.

Country correspondence, if nothing else, is *personal* journalism. It gives weather reports, but with something besides temperatures and forecasts. From Grandma Wilma, one of my favorites, out at Tapps Ridge:

> Hello friends and neighbors, how are you this beautiful Monday evening? Hope you are all well and able to enjoy this beautiful weather we are having. It is really a lovely time of year—great for traveling, visiting the parks, and going to ball games at the schools. Hope you enjoyed the World Series. Grandma Wilma did. I was cheering for the Phillies but they lost. Anyway it was nice to watch it on TV. This is porch weather for Grandma Wilma.

Occasionally, you get a bit of philosophizing.

> Having raised two baby kittens with a medicine dropper after their mother was killed this spring, I wonder if they might be a bit like teenagers. They play and have a great time, will eat potato chips and drink chocolate milk and I'm sure they'd like hamburgers and French fries. They have their share of fun and the Borgmans enjoy watching them.

Public service is performed.

> There is a baking dish with lid at the Cross Plains Baptist Church left from a "carry-in" at the annual association meeting last month at the Cross Plains church. The owner will possibly need it for Thanksgiving. Please call me and we will see that it gets home.

These folk live with wildlife close by and the accounts reflect the joy and tragedy of all God's creatures mingled together.

> At our house the mocking bird trills his beautiful songs morning and evening. He is a joy to hear.

> I miss the big spider on top of the Indian mound this year. But with the corn there, maybe you couldn't see it from the road this year.

Most of our doings and minor misfortunes are too tame to make the columns of bigger newspapers or get on television news. From time to time some tv station will do a feature about one of our artisans who makes beer-can sculptures and we get into the roundups of regional news in the metropolitan press. We don't have many big crime cases but when we do, they are grisly and shocking. Then we get a taste of media frenzy and Main Street will be crowded with television vans with their satellite uplink dishes, embarrassing us with unwanted attention.

It's a space-time problem; by the time the media has covered the hurricanes and earthquakes, murders and sex crimes, layoffs and takeovers, wars and politics and so on there isn't room for much else. News is, by definition, the exceptional, the unusual. We are exposed to so much of it compressed into news reports that we assume the exception is the rule, and we are scared by it. In the real world, most of the time most of the people go about the work and worry of their daily lives feeling joy or concern over little-noticed breaks in routine—a birthday party, a bout with cancer, trading in the old car for a new one, supper at the Griffins. That may not be news, but it is reality.

Country correspondents serve well reporting on that reality. And encouraging us to have a care for each other.

Lucy Brown was moved to the Clifty Falls Convalescent Center on Tuesday. Her pneumonia seems to be clear but the stroke has left her partially paralyzed. She does not talk but opens her eyes when anyone takes hold of her hand.

Lucy knows she is not forgotten. That's a comfort to her and worthy of us.

Jennifer Shulz is about the same.

GEORGE

# The First Book of George

Our night visitor is out there again. The beagle with one torn ear now joins us when we come out for the morning run, greeting Amigo with such fresh enthusiasm you'd never guess he had escorted us home from our night walk a few hours before.

He emerges from the backyard so he must have slept in the doghouse. Mary will like that. She acquired the doghouse from some petless people willing to give it to anyone who would haul it away. It was to be shelter for Amigo if a rain came up, but now has an occasional overnight occupant.

The beagle is either a free roaming spirit or a homeless stray. He cleans up the leftovers in Amigo's dishes and food I put out for him is always gone in the morning. He obviously approves of the food and the accommodations but he's only a transient guest.

I've asked around and the neighbors are familiar with the beagle but nobody knows where he belongs. One man thought his name was George. I tried it on him and he didn't seem to know or care what he was called. He just likes attention, especially from Amigo.

They are a mismatch. Amigo, tall, svelte, ears up sharp, graceful. George, short by comparison but big for a beagle, husky, ears flopped down, moving with purpose and muscular power from hind quarters that remind me of a race horse. What they share is a mysterious past, unknown to me but perhaps it unites them in some way.

When he's around, George joins excursions of the Marching and Sniffing Society, increasing its membership to five. We start out with Amigo and George. At the old farmhouse on the city limits we pick up Boomer and Red. Red is an old dog of indefinable breed, short, stout, reddish brown. Boomer is of equally unknown parentage, tiny, quick, multicolored, the best hunter of the lot. Red and George don't like each other, a natural personality clash. They growl and circle and threaten when they meet, then agree to disagree and avoid each other.

A quarter mile farther along the county road by the river we sometimes pick up Lady, a German shepherd belonging to Don Thompson, a towboater who works out of Bennett's Landing. Lady suffers from indecision and distrust, comes out barking and acts as if she'd like to join us, but isn't sure. Sometimes she does, sometimes she doesn't.

The parade moves east, exploring as it moves but making steady progress forward. Amigo and Boomer lead, Red sticks close to me, George covers the rear with Lady farther behind, trying to decide whether to come along. They take my directions so agreeably I doubt anyone would believe five dogs can be controlled almost as easily as one.

We prowl along the river bank, poke into the brush lining the runoff ponds, pass the docks and barges at the Landing, work our way into the woods and fields beyond. Little Boomer turns up the most scents and will burrow furiously after an unseen critter. George usually pulls up late, but he is just as eager investigating a cooled-off trail. Amigo's attention span is short so she moves on quickly looking for new game.

It's a sight when some brave creature shows itself, a rabbit maybe or ground hog. Off goes the whole Society chasing madly, some not sure what. Not that it matters. They seldom catch anything but spending one's self in a lost cause can be redemptive.

George's hunting skills show lack of training or experience with other beagles. He backtracks on a scent, runs with nose-down tail-up intensity after where the prey came from, not where it is headed. Even Boomer knows better. You can't fault George for his work ethic though; he's the last to give up.

Strays like George are self educated and he has done well. He covers much more ground than the others yet never tires because he's learned to conserve energy. He uses the shortest, easiest route, runs along the roadway when the rest of us are plodding through brush. This worried me until I discovered how streetwise he is. He can detect an oncoming vehicle by sound as much as sight and avoids it without seeming to notice. He has an obsession with some trucks, gets downright indignant, takes after them in a fury. Others don't bother him. I watched with fear and amazement when he took on a huge semitrailer rig, tore alongside the cab just giving the beast hell.

As loners must, George has learned how to amuse himself. The river fascinates him. He stands in the shallow water's edge, not getting his belly wet, and watches the swirls and ripples, never moving. When wind or barges make waves, he stands captivated by the flow lapping into a culvert and out again, his head following the movement of the water back and forth, back and forth.

We reach the end of our course, a couple miles from home, and turn back. On the return trip, the Society members drop off at their home bases. Lady first, if she has come along, because her place comes up first. Then Boomer peels off, but Red passes his house and hangs with us for a quarter mile or so, reluctant to leave such agreeable company. When we reach the road up to the President Madison Motel, I turn, put up a hand in a blocking gesture and say, "Go home, Red. We'll see you tomorrow." Red stares at me for a moment, then turns and toddles on home.

Amigo is ready for a nap when we get home. George checks

out the food dishes, then goes back outside. He may just be an outside dog, not accustomed to confinement. Beagles are roamers and he probably has more business on his agenda. When I look for him again, he has disappeared.

A week or two may go by before we see him again. On night walks, Amigo will lead me to the house where George hangs out, looking for him. He's not always there but when he is, he follows us home and stays a few days.

I miss him when he's not around, but in a way I'm relieved. If the neighbors see him with me all the time, there could be the devil to pay.

I mean, how can they hold you responsible for a dog that doesn't have a collar, or a name for sure, and is known all over this end of town as a stray? When you come down to it, George is simply not my dog.

# 7 The Peril of Righteousness

My exoneration by Mr. Justice Hoying on the trumped-up charge of allowing an animal to run loose encouraged me in the conviction that Truth protects the pure of heart. Succeeding events reaffirmed that conviction.

The first came at the laundromat, that center of social discourse, education, entertainment and self-service cleanliness. One I frequent holds poetry readings. At another, women of country-western inclination bring in their instruments on Thursday mornings and engage us all with a bit of pickin' and singin' while articles of apparel slosh and tumble.

The laundromat is also a source of fairly reliable gossip. Thus I learned of the extra-policing activities of the officer who was my nemesis in the off-leash affair. He was reported to be hitting on the blonde clerk at the minimarket next door; his cruiser was seen parked there for unusually long periods. It required only a few sly inquires to recreate events of that morning prior to when I was so falsely accused. He had been goofing off, needed a bust to show for his time, and I was it.

Later came a newspaper report of Officer Nemesis being charged with misappropriating funds entrusted to him by some organization. He copped a plea and escaped doing time but was dismissed from the force. I encountered him one time after that, clerking in an appliance store. He avoided me.

As I pulled weeds in the yard one afternoon while Amigo watched, I was approached by Mrs. Gray, an elderly widow from down the street with whom I had exchanged pleasantries. "I didn't know that was *your* dog," she blurted out, then confessed it was she who had called the law to report that some stray dog was in her yard. She apologized sincerely, said she didn't want me to get the wrong idea.

Justified by faith. I felt almost as if I <u>belonged</u>.

My next-door neighbors are friendly for the most part; we talk across the fence as we work in the yard. Three adults and assorted children. A small boy and a girl, they can't be more than four and five, excitedly call "Here doggie" to Amigo, who comes to the fence to allow her nose to be touched through the wire. She is even more friendly with the teenage girl, who sometimes comes around on the street side to see Amigo, talks to her and rubs her behind the ears. The girl wants a dog of her own badly but her father refuses. I see him seldom; he is usually scowling.

One mild Saturday afternoon I was flopped on the couch watching a football game when my stupor was dissipated by the wail of sirens coming closer, growing louder, then ceasing abruptly, <u>here</u>! My door was open and Amigo was nowhere in sight. I rushed to the street to find a crowd gathering, drawn by two police cars and the dogcatcher's truck that were pulled up in front of the house next door. In the backyard one cop and the dogcatcher, who was brandishing a long pole with a looped rope on the end, were closing in on Amigo, trapped in a corner by the fence and a shed.

She was relieved to see me coming to her rescue. A police officer followed as I took Amigo home, past the neighbors muttering among themselves. He was almost apologetic about the excessive-force strike to capture a dog who had strayed where it didn't belong. Almost reluctantly he wrote out a citation. I made no attempt at a defense. How could I, with Amigo caught in the act?

This time when I appeared before the bar of justice court was in session. I sat in the back through almost three hours of cases. My offense had little standing compared to possession of marijuana, unsafe start and theft of property under $100.

The docket was finished and court all but cleared before Judge Hoying acknowledged me as a pleasant surprise. "Mr. Spaid, what are you doing here?"

"Same old thing," I said, puzzled and a tad offended that the court had no record, the judge was uninformed of my flagrant offense. It fell to me to explain my presence, to describe my transgression. I did so truthfully, putting the best possible face on it.

The judge listened patiently, with some amusement, as I hung myself. I complained mildly about the absence of court records, of no prosecuting witness. He said this was only a quasijudicial matter. I argued entrapment, my dog having been lured next door by the entreaties of younger parties at the residence. The judge chuckled.

"I'd be inclined to let you off if you hadn't been watching tv," he said, reinforcing everything I had heard of the evils of television. It was up to me; if I wanted to plead guilty, he'd fine me $1 and costs.

I copped that plea, not knowing that the costs would run $33 and the court wouldn't take a check.

# 8 A Home of Her Own

We are fencing in the backyard, Robert Frost notwithstanding. The poet had his doubts about whether "Good fences make good neighbors." It came up while he and his neighbor were repairing a section of their common fence knocked down by hunters. The neighbor recited the homily as wisdom handed down, unexamined, from his father. Poet Frost wasn't so certain and asked, in that perspicacious manner poets have: "Isn't it where there are cows? But there are no cows here. Before I built a wall I'd ask to know what I was walling in or walling out and to whom I was like to give offense."

There are no cows here either, and I tend to agree with the poet's principle of asking to know the purpose of a fence. For pastures and penitentiaries, yes, but barricades between neighbors may not be appropriate in an open society. Still, residential fences have long been popular, if only for decoration. In Madison's early building era, some lovely wrought-iron creations were forged in the town's own foundries, which cast ironworks for commerce. Afterward came wide-squared wire, waist high, and then the tight-webbed chain link, when aesthetics gave way to security. Now going up all over town are the close-boarded, can't-see-over "privacy" fences. We are boarding in and boarding out.

Our own fence building is not entirely because of my run-in with the law and the neighbors. In fact, the woman from next door sought me out and apologized for bringing down the full force of the town's law enforcement on bewildered Amigo. Her dog-hater husband did it.

As relief from my ungreen years in high-rise apartments, I have become outside caretaker—mowing the lawn, planting flower beds, raking leaves, replenishing bird feeders. Mary supplies materials, I the sweat equity. We struck the same bargain on enclosing the backyard—it was already fenced on two sides—to make a secure place to leave Amigo outside.

Mary brought in sturdy logs for posts and wire fencing from her tree farm and Gary, the tenant on the place and a turn-to guy who can make or fix anything, helped stretch the fence and built a gate. I dug the holes and set the posts, a job that took time, perspiration and swearing.

The swearing was mostly at Fritz, a dachshund from across the alley who took umbrage at my working so close by his turf and let me know it. (I feel sorry for Fritz; he never gets any respect. He barks at all who approach but a dachshund's size and sound are so puny, nobody pays any attention.)

I was stretching and grunting after the hard-packed dirt at the bottom of a deep hole one morning, ignoring Fritz' yapping, when out of raw frustration he lunged at me. He didn't even get in a bite; from nowhere Amigo came running and sent Fritz yelping for home.

I not only have an amigo, I have a protector. I will reciprocate; the new enclave will protect her from the neighborhood predators and long runs where humans seldom venture will satisfy her wanderlust.

One of those refuges is the ridge above the Hillside Inn, a motel on a shelf high above the town and valley, only three blocks away. A winding drive leads up the hill to the Inn; from that level an access road climbs steeply to the City's water reservoir, a huge buried bubble. Even in this remoteness there are marks of civilization; the low rounded roof of the reservoir is covered with graffiti. Most is of the Rob-Loves-Nina and Tracey-&-Damon-4-Ever genre, work of the lovestruck. Four-letter or two-word vulgarisms are few but there are many scrawled initials, products of the universal urge to leave one's mark on the world.

From the reservoir plateau a steep, narrow footpath runs up the ridge, a good quarter mile of climbing. It takes half an hour and one needs to start down in time to reach bottom before dark. Tramping around lost in the blackness can be scary; I've learned to let Amigo lead.

She is alert to the prospects about, may disappear up the slope above the path or plunge into the ravine below after a scent or a sound. She has flushed rabbits, possum, deer, squirrels, raccoon, once a coyote. I've stood perfectly still while she drove a rabbit right to me; one ran across my foot.

The path runs out near the top, blocked by a tall cliff ahead.

To the left 100 feet above the trail you emerge from the wood into the rolling meadow of a farm, with outbuildings in the distance. Amigo explores here but I perch on a rock on the trail below. Serenity time for me, tuned to the frequency of the forest—wind shushing in the leaves, trees groaning, birds fluttering and calling overhead.

No climb of the ridge is like another. Wildflowers are profuse in their time, but change hue subtly from sun to shade. A tree is newly fallen across the path, felled by wind or lightning. Water sometimes flows freely from rock to rock, at other times trickles. When we are hot and thirsty, the bed is dry. New-growth branches slap my arms. On a muggy day spider webs spun across the trail annoy my face and hair. One time the path is slippery, treacherous, next time boot-deep in leaves.

Amigo peers down on me from a precipice, tall and alert, posing. The offer of an oatmeal cookie brings her to me and we snack, but soon she whines to get going. The trip down is easier, unless rains have made the path muddy. Here is where the four-legged mammal shows man, full of superiority since he first stood upright, that two legs furnish only uncertain footing on the earth.

Part way down we have a choice: we can retrace our route to the Inn, rounding the ridge through a parking lot to a fresh purlieu with a deep-bank creek and, when running, a waterfall just high enough to be heard. Or we can reach the place climbing over the top of the ridge and down. It's slow, hard going that way through a thicket of bramble bushes. I struggle to pull free of sticking branches and wonder why we came this way. Amigo loves it; the briar patch is a rabbit haven.

She was with me when we started down. I saw her emerging from the brambles. Now she's disappeared.

At the bottom I wait, scan the hill for her black image. I give her more time, then call.

She could have scented a rabbit and given chase. I wait a while longer.

Come on, Amigo. I call several times, trying to throw my voice up the hill.

I check my watch; almost fifteen minutes have gone by. This isn't like her. I'm getting worried.

I climb the hill, toward where I saw her last. At the brambles I call repeatedly. "Amigo. Here, girl. Where are you?" I visualize her emerging from the brush.

She could have gone back down the other side, chasing something. Or made her own way to the car in the lot by the Inn. I stumble back down the hill, hurry around to the Inn. No sign of her.

For two hours I search, scramble up, over, around the hill, expecting, hoping to come upon her. My voice is hoarse. It will be dark in another hour. Could she have fallen, be lying hurt and helpless?

Could Mary's retrievers find her? It's worth a try. I hurry to the car and drive to Mary's. She's confident Smiling Sam and Butterscotch Candy can scent Amigo. She loads them in her car and follows me back to the Inn.

The retrievers are excited and willing but uncertain of the task. They come bounding after as I climb the hill where I last saw Amigo. I call her name, hoping to convey my purpose to them. I entreat Sam, "Go find Amigo." His tail lashes wildly in eagerness. Scotch is poking into bushes.

I lead them around the base of the hill, down into a creek gorge, stop, yell Amigo's name, demonstrating what I want of them. They scurry about as if on the hunt, but after a time it is evident they are searching for anything they can turn up, not Amigo.

They follow me less closely, finally make their way back down to Mary. After a last look in the dusk, I return to Mary and the dogs.

"You might as well go home," I tell her.

She tries to be reassuring. "She may come home on her own."

"I'd better check." On the way home, I slowly drive the streets that we have often walked home from the Inn. At home, no Amigo.

For the rest of the day's light, I search the neighborhood, driving a widening pattern between home and the Inn. No trace.

I stop at the minimarket, where Amigo has gone with me, to ask if they might have seen her. No, the woman behind the counter says, but she is so concerned I am touched.

Dark now, useless to look for a black dog. The thought of Amigo out there in the night, somewhere, maybe hurt, is painful. I vow to start again first thing in the morning.

My mind won't quit exploring possibilities. Maybe she has been picked up. I call the police station. A man with a husky voice answers. "No," he says gently, "we've had no report on a dog like that picked up." Then sympathetically, "But we'll sure keep a look out for her."

There is nothing more I can do. A fantasy of finding her fills my thoughts, so I feel the relief. Then reality returns. I haven't eaten but I am not hungry. Television doesn't distract me.

Gradually, I accept my own reassurance that I will find her in the morning. Then I hear, behind me, the slurp, slurp, slurp of a dog drinking water from the dish by the open door. It's Amigo!

She's almost too tired to do more than wag her tail slightly to greet me. I can feel her heart beating hard as I hug her.

I talk to her, tell her how worried I've been, how long I looked. She listens patiently, then heads for the bedroom and flops into her corner, as if to say that rest, not reassurance is what she needs.

I leave her to sleep, elated that she is back.

She found her way. She knows where home is.

# 9 A Vociferous Charade

My favorite bird, next to the sparrow, is the killdeer. I have an egalitarian affiliation with the sparrow, which I regard as the common man of the bird population. An ordinary working stiff.

To paraphrase, God must have loved the sparrow because He made so many of them. They are everywhere, working harder than other birds to get their share of whatever is to be got, usually leftovers. They have better table manners when they share the seed I throw out on the driveway than uncouth blue jays or bickering doves, or fat-bellied blackbirds or even the squirrel from across the street who carefully picks out the sunflower seeds and leaves the rest, like the guest at a cocktail party who eats only the cashews in the nut dishes. The sparrow takes what's left and never complains.

The sparrow is also snubbed by bird people, too unexotic to bear watching, never the hero in children's books, doesn't even rate a separate listing in the bird book but is thrown in with grosbeaks, finches and buntings and is ignominiously described as a "sooty city bird" with "a plain dingy breast and dull eye-stripe." True, no merchandiser of cutesy collectibles ever struck a limited-edition plate of the sparrow. He is too unlimited.

In spite of his nondescript appearance, the sparrow bravely rises above his station with a cheery, quite melodious song, as if to console himself for the injustices of the pecking order while he scratches out a living. Let's back him up with a few bars of Copeland's "Fanfare for the Common Man."

The killdeer has more going for him. His appearance is quite striking, his dull brown body set off by a white nose, throat and belly and black rings around the collar. He has bent gull wings, like the old Corsair Navy fighter plane, ornamentally traced in white.

He can run almost as fast as he flies, in a flat-out line with spindly legs churning to a blurr. I've had one run along ahead of me for 30 yards or so when I'm jogging at the water's edge and outrun me.

Killdeer hang out by gravel roads, build a nest in the open near the road, then devote much of their existence to defending it. And defend it they do, employing a scold-and-divert tactic. When you come near—oddly, they will let you walk very close—they fuss at you, really raise ned. If scolding doesn't work, they try diversion, fly at you and away, taunting you to chase after.

For once, the scientific name of a bird is of significance to someone besides an ornithology major writing a term paper. The killdeer is *charadrius vociferous*, which freely translates as vociferous charade—an apt description of the desperate act he puts on when all else fails. He plays wounded, flips one wing up over his back and flaps the ground with the other furiously, screaming bloody murder all the time. It is quite a performance, intended to draw your attention away from the nest. If you're not prepared for this ruse, it can be a small horror show.

We frequently encounter killdeer on our treks, noisy when the dogs draw near but not altogether unfriendly, almost welcoming. I try to reassure  them that we are just passing through and won't bother them. Sometimes they stop jabbering and listen, then go right back to their tirade.

Most of the dogs are uninterested, but now let us bring in one who is—by pedigree named Serindipity Samantha, but by common sense called Rennie. Remember I told you that Mary is a nut about golden retrievers; she has always had one, now has two. Even so, when the vet told her of a six-month-old fullblood needing a home because her owners travel a lot, Mary was hooked. And then she had three.

Rennie is a tan, small-bodied core of hyperkenetic mischief who looks on life as play-play-play. Eats enough for three dogs, hers and theirs. Ready to detonate out any door that's opened a crack. She ignores the seniority rights of Smiling Sam and Butterscotch Candy, pestering them to play, but they mostly ignore her and find a safe corner to sleep.

Mary made an effort at the obligatory obedience training with Rennie and gave her up as hopeless. Too much uncontainable energy. So when I offered to take Rennie along on our outings and run some of that excess out of her, Mary agreed with relief.

It is an envy to observe all that vitality. Rennie wants to be everywhere at once and almost is, running from me to the other dogs ahead or behind or off in some thicket, then back to me. She craves physical contact, bumps against my leg periodically to impress on me that she's there. Once when I was running she knocked my grounded leg out from under me and sent me sprawling; I should have penalized her for blindsiding.

Match all that enthusiasm with the frenetic activity of the killdeer and you have a spectacle. Rennie is a sucker for their flyby taunts to chase them and she takes the bait every time. One will swoop down, screech at Rennie, and off they go—the killdeer flying low to the ground and out of reach but close enough to keep Rennie tempted.

She never comes close to catching up with any of the birds, but she never stops trying. And they use reinforcements; when one gets tired, another takes over running Rennie ragged. She never learns, every rematch the birds get the best of it.

One evening up at Bennett's Landing a particularly cagy killdeer put the tease on Rennie, who took the challenge, bounding headlong after the bird flying low toward a dock on the river. The killdeer swooped to the end of the dock and out over the river. Racing heedlessly after, Rennie suddenly realized her plight and slammed on the brakes. She planted all four legs, strained back against her momentum, and skidded to a stop inches from the edge of the dock and the water below. It was a Tom and Jerry cartoon.

Once we came upon the killdeer family that lives by the storage domes of the grain terminal. They were unusually edgy, three of them, darting at the dogs and at me, imploring us to give chase. We didn't but as I approached one on the ground a few feet ahead, he went into his wounded-bird act, thrashing and shrieking. Then he ran from me a way, beckoning me to follow, offering himself as a sacrifice. To the side, another shrilled at me.

Then I saw them, three small killdeer babies, walking slowly in an unstable line from the mother who was scolding me. Miniatures of their parents, quite unaware of any danger.

I steered the dogs away and around the killdeer and their young and as we drew away, the din ceased. Now I knew what all the fuss was about.

SANDY

# 10 Sandy

The trauma of divorce can drive people to the crazies. One couple I knew who prided themselves on the maturity with which they worked through the quagmire of the property settlement came to a painting that he said was his and she said he gave her as a gift—and they were mature no longer. Another pair decided who got what with uncommon equanimity, only to have all hell break loose over which could keep a golf bag.

Possession of a pet has been known to stir almost as much contention as the custody of children. In one horrifying case, a couple was so unrelenting in refusing to allow the other to keep the family dog that they agreed to have it put to sleep.

A more humane resolution of such a conflict was devised by two people I was close to who were in divorce proceedings. They had a dog, a striking white German shepherd that neither wanted the other to have. Since I was a dog person and "neutral," would I keep the dog until they could work out a final agreement?

I really didn't need another dog, what with the neighbors alert to any of Amigo's transgressions and George hanging around enough for them to believe he was mine. It crossed my mind that this interim arrangement could become permanent. But, I took in Sandy as a refugee from a broken home.

She adjusted quickly, apparently preferred canine bickering

to human, and there was some. Twice furious fights broke out when I put Amigo and Sandy in the backyard. Two German shepherds tearing into each other set off an alarming uproar that brought me on the run. I pulled at them and scared them apart by the sheer harshness of my shouting, a sign they half welcomed my intervention. Both brawls were brief and no damage was done. Those outbursts settled the hierarchical matter; Sandy accepted her follower place behind Amigo the leader.

If anything, Sandy is too docile. She is the compliant child in a family who strives tirelessly to please and cringes in remorse at scolding. Call her "Bad Dog" and she slinks away, ears depressed, and sulks. Minutes later she comes fawning to win her way back into favor.

Sandy's a "leaner," an excessively dependent creature who must be in the same room with me, who won't eat until she knows I'm not likely to leave. She watches me constantly. No sense of humor, can't take kidding, is uncertain about affection and has to be talked into play.

Perhaps this is because Sandy was a foundling, picked up on the loose as an abandoned puppy. Mary has a theory that a pup separated from its nurturing mother in the early weeks of life and with no human surrogate will be an insecure dog the rest of its life.

Sandy has her qualities. She's a looker, a sloe-eyed dazzler who draws those "Pretty dog!" accolades that white shepherds do. She's not all white; up close she shows a tannish sandy cast along back and shoulders. So she's aptly named.

They are a matched set, Sandy and Amigo, almost identical, one white, one black, salt and pepper.

Amigo is the more graceful; Sandy's walk is a waddle with a side-to-side hip swing; I sometimes call her "Wigglebutt." Where she puts Amigo to shame is in the river. Sandy grew up in Florida and learned to swim in the ocean. She takes to water like the ducks on the river and sometimes paddles with them, or swims along as I walk the bank. Amigo is a wader; she cools her feet and laps a drink, but goes in only up to her chest.

George is a bit water wary too, a stander; he appreciates water for its taste and air-conditioning, but doesn't care to get his belly wet.

One day I returned to the car from the store and found Sandy barking excitedly, head out the back window, looking up. High above the roof of the store drifted a blue-striped hot-air balloon. She has a fetish about prominent objects overhead. Once she barked up a hissy fit at the end of the driveway. Looking toward the river I could see why; an enormous red-yellow-black balloon rising up almost ominously then floating gradually back down. Some entrepreneur on the riverbank was giving customers rides.

Her fixation can go too far. A used-car dealer trying to attract attention sent up a bright orange balloon on a tether. Sandy gave it what-for, not only when she saw it but for days after it was gone when we passed that way. At night she is sometimes offended by headlights of cars on the bridge, or street lights. One mellow evening she broke the calm with an off-key, insistent but plaintive barking, sitting at the end of the driveway. Through the trees across the street, hanging massive and low, was the moon.

Sandy's otherwise meek personality has an incongruous strain; she's a hunter, with a killer instinct. Amigo and George are primarily scenters and chasers; it is Sandy who moves in for the kill. She is skilled and mercifully quick, grabs a fat ground hog behind the head, shakes hard and sharp and snaps out life.

She has a penchant for snakes, seeks them out in the spring when they are small. Garter or cow snakes mostly, but she's turned up copperheads. Instinct serves well; she darts in, grabs swiftly and shakes with a fury, so the snake has no chance to bite. I don't share her attitude about reptiles, so I usually call her off. Still, it's comforting to know she's on the lookout.

The woods behind the Milton sewage plant on the Kentucky side of the river is one of our escapes, a four-block drive from home. The ATV drivers have cut a trail a couple miles deep on the slant of hills rising from the gorge of a winding creek that is a dry rocky trench most of the year but can swell to river size in high water. The trail is as wide as the wheelbase of the three or four-wheel all-terrain vehicles, the recreational vehicle of choice in these parts.

The drone of the ATVs intrudes on the stillness of the forest but the noise warns us they are coming, often in a parade of four or five. Our encounters are unfailingly congenial; the riders have come to know me and the dogs and there is a comradely spirit among people who meet in the wild. We cooperate; they cut the trail and I pull down limbs and break off tall brush that hangs at face level.

We follow the ATV trail to where it turns around, then wade the undergrowth beyond to a briarpatch rabbit warren and a swampy bog that can turn up turtles or muskrats. Amigo and George range out of sight but Sandy sticks by me, until George sounds off that they're onto something, then she thrashes off to join the hunt.

When the scent has been worked to no avail, we settle on a high bank of the creek and rest, or at least I do. They wade or prowl until I am renewed enough to start back. We cross the creek, an opportunity for them to demonstrate their superiority in climbing steep banks. We follow the hedgerows along the creek, skirting fields of farms with buildings in the distance; the resident dog warns us off.

In one of those fields Sandy made her find. I saw her cautiously feigning at some critter, thrust and back off, then thrust again. Closer in I could see the high bushy tail, then the telltale black and white stripes on its back—a skunk!

Heedlessly, stupidly, Sandy stalked her prey. Dart in, jump back. Once she grabbed it up, shook it furiously, then flung it away. The skunk made no effort to flee, stood defiantly, back arched. Sandy went after it again.

I can't say I saw the skunk fire its salvo of acrid spray, but I sure as hell smelled it. In the excitement of the fray, the dumb dog ignored the stench until I called her off. Only then did she realize that she had been doused, and retreated.

I led her away—from several paces in front. The skunk stood still for a time, then disappeared in the weeds.

I made for the creek, Sandy following meekly, stinkingly, behind. The creekbed was mostly dry but I found a pool of standing water. Sandy needed no instruction; she plunged in, immersed herself as much as she could.

Amigo and George arrived to see what was up, no doubt drawn by an unmistakable scent. They stood off on the bank observing. The creek bath helped little. Stronger measures were called for so we headed for the car.

The dogs took their usual places, George in front next to me, Amigo and Sandy in back. Amigo immediately stuck her head out her window and kept it there. I rolled down the rest of the windows, opened the air vents.

I stopped at a grocery store and bought big cans of tomato juice and a large bottle of lemon juice, ingredients for skunk deodorizing I'd read about.

At home I banished Sandy to the backyard until I could fill the bathtub. When I led her in and put her in the tub she resisted not at all. I lathered her thoroughly, rinsed, then lathered and rinsed again. She stood stoical, with her bad-dog look. I drenched her with the tomato juice, rubbed until her white hair turned crimson. Then the lemon juice, poured on, rubbed in. She made only a feeble attempt to shake off when I took her out and consigned her to the backyard to dry off.

It took days for the effect of Sandy's encounter with the skunk to wear off; not the odor, which vanished almost completely in a few hours. Maybe the stinker struck her a glancing blow or didn't loose a full load. It was the blemish to her pride that remained.

She was humiliated, hesitated to respond to any overture as if she wasn't deserving of attention. I imagined the other dogs might be avoiding her, but they paid her no more or less attention than they had before.

After several days of coaxing, extra bones, rides alone with me to the grocery store and continuous talking to, she began to regain her self esteem. When she growled off Amigo for even looking at a bone she was guarding between her paws, I figured she was back to her old neurotic self. Now all she needed was a crash course in animal identification.

# The Second Book of George

Whenever I complain to Mary and Georgia about my growing menagerie of dogs and what the neighbors are apt to make of that, I get precious little sympathy. "I am just *keeping* Sandy," I say and Georgia just smiles. "I didn't *adopt* George," I insist and Mary chuckles. "No, you didn't. He adopted you."

I'm stuck. Amigo and Sandy are not the problem; they're controllable, at least within reach of control. George is an itinerant, here part of the time and gone part of the time. No use trying to pen him up; put him in the backyard and he leaps up on the roof of the doghouse and launches himself over the fence. Chaining him would be contrary to his instinct and experience; he's a beagle and a stray.

He survived in the years before he took up lodgings with me with nobody watching over him but God. Of course, that's it. I have temporary custody of Sandy. I will share custody of George with his Heavenly Master.

The joint-custody arrangement would be quite simple; when George is on the premises, I will be in charge and when he leaves, God takes over. Of course, I must give notice of the transfer. When I see George take off or when he doesn't respond to my call, I pray, "Well, Lord, he's in Your hands now. Please take care of him."

I feel a certain comfort in the arrangement. My only misgiving is a suspicion that some of my neighbors and the dogcatcher may not be true believers.

One day when we were patrolling for critters above the Hillside Inn I got a glimpse of how George made it on his own. As he did his customary inspection of the garbage cans outside the kitchen door of the Inn, two white-uniformed workers came out. They greeted George, and he them, like old buddies. They had obviously been slipping him handouts—doing the work of the Lord.

Not that George would live on handouts; he has the work ethic of a Puritan. Hunting is his vocation, what he was put on earth for. Sleeping and eating are merely preparation for his mission. When we run the shoreline downriver—past the junkyard, sewage treatment plant, grain terminal, old refinery and country club golf course to the power plant–he has places that require checking all along the way, like a night watchman punching in at stations along his rounds. He ventures at some distance from the more-or-less straightaway path that I take or Amigo, who explores randomly within a shout and Sandy, who stays in sight unless something interesting turns up.

Merely covering his assigned territory takes time enough, but if George encounters anything amiss, say a rabbit loitering in a clump, then time is suspended. He may howl for help on the move, bringing Amigo and Sandy charging. After some excited darting around, they come back to me but George stays on the scent long after it has faded. He may pick it up again, set to howling and off they go on another wild-rabbit chase.

I trace George out on the horizon by sound mostly, see him emerge from a woods into a clearing, then disappear again. He is more visible in winter through the bare limbs and his beagle bark carries clearer in the cold air. He may range for miles, slip along the creek and under the highway overpass bridge up into the high forest of the State Hospital grounds.

Then I must revert to the traditional hunter-hound communication, listening for his periodic far-off howls, that arching melodic sonance which blesses the human ear like no other sound.

If I don't hear him for a time and look to see him appear, it is never where I expect. I don't find George; he finds me. One damp autumn day on the Sunrise Golf Course when Sandy and Amigo had had their run and it was time to leave I spent half an hour calling and whistling into the ravine where George was last heard from. I sat on a log to rest and wonder how long the wait would be this time, felt a sudden pounce on my back. It was George, out of nowhere, wiggling happily as if to ask, "Where have you been?"

When we go in the car, we park the same place at each site—the golf-course parking lot, the boat-launching ramp by the bridge, the drive to the sewage-treatment plant, which, by the way, is odiferous only in a downwind stream of air that can be quickly crossed. It is agreed that we will meet at the car after, the way families do who go separate ways at the state fair or a ball game. After an hour of hunt and run Sandy and Amigo are pooped enough to head back to the car, gladly crawl into their seats. George is another matter.

He may have made his presence known not far back, or may not. Then begins calling time, when I shout and whistle to summon George. I've gotten pretty good at whistling, able to project for distance, how effectively I can't tell. I usually give it 20 or 30 minutes, at intervals, while grumbling to Amigo and Sandy, who are amazingly patient. If George shows up, he jumps into the front seat with a glow of excitement that melts my consternation. If not, we often drive to the grocery store, pick up a few supplies, then return and give George another try. If we're running on the Kentucky side of the river I may take Amigo and Sandy home, feed them, then go back after George, usually find him hanging around the meeting place, wondering where I've been.

He may not turn up at all. When I have to give up and leave without him, I always feel I'm betraying him. He knows the way home, can follow the river bank or the valley of Crooked Creek from the golf course, an expedition that may take three days to cover thoroughly. When he's gone for days like that I figure it's because the Lord loves George's company.

When he shows up, it is the return of the prodigal and I feel like the father who killed the fatted calf, except it is only a juicy bone.

George is an ardent follower of the commandment, Love Thy Neighbor. Especially his canine neighbors; particularly female canine neighbors.

If he is absent for more than a week and someone asks about him I always say, "He's got a girl friend." No more needs be said.

Once in a while, driving around, I'll catch a glimpse of him in hot pursuit of an appealing bitch, along with other suitors, or camped out on the doorstep of his lady love, plighting his troth. No point in trying to dissuade him for the mundane offerings of home; food doesn't matter, sleep doesn't matter—love is all.

I once tried to pick him up and carry him home and did him a disservice. A rival suitor named Tiger, with a disposition to match, attacked George, dangling in my arms, and bit him on the leg.

What with his hunting responsibilities and his amorous adventures, George is away a lot, although he sticks around as much as he can. After all, he never had a home before.

When he disappears, I play a time game. I give him 48 to 72 hours to come home on his own, then begin cruising around looking for him. I have five to seven days to call the dog pound to see if he has been picked up before they exterminate him, depending on the day of the week; death takes weekends off.

If he has eluded the dogcatcher, then I have to allow three

weeks for the time of a female's heat before figuring he has gone for good. It never takes that long. Twice I have bailed him out of the slammer; once for being loose and once for being even looser, caught in the act of love with a lady beagle, reported by some unromantic citizen.

The animal control officer doesn't call when George is picked up even though my name and phone number are on his collar. I can't complain because with my rap sheet I'd get cited again and the fall for two-time loser is fierce. So I settle for paying George's keep and a pickup fee and keep my mouth shut.

We've had a change in the town's political administration so we have a new dogcatcher and he paid me a visit. It was not a social call. He said he'd gotten complaints (plural) about my dogs (plural) running loose all over the neighborhood. He wouldn't say what dog, or where the crime occurred, or who reported it.

He is skinny and wimpy, speaks in a voice so weak I can hardly hear him and says the least he can. I am outraged at being accused with no bill of particulars. I fume about the right of every American to confront his accuser and he says only, "I'm just doing my job." I invoke presumption of innocence. He listens blankly, then replies, "I'm just doing my job."

"How do you know it was one of my dogs?" I demand, but he just shakes his head. "What do you mean, complaints? Where? When? Who?"

"I don't know," he replies. "Just somebody called the law."

My fulminations must have had some effect because he wrote out what he said was "only a warning. But if it happens again, you'll have to go to court." Even that seemed flimsy and unjust, but I shut up. He was new and didn't know I was not a first offender.

For months I saw him driving by the house in that white truck with the cage in the back. Or parked under the bridge when we went out for our morning run. He would grin sheepishly and say nothing, just watch and wait. I was under official surveillance now, besides being under the sharp eye of the neighbors.

It was enough to make a man paranoid. I even got a little peeved at the Lord, Who was supposed to be looking out for George when I couldn't. That was the agreement.

I remembered the story of the farmer who had planted and tended a plot set aside as God's Acre, its produce to be given to the church as the farmer's tithe. The preacher dropped by one day, stood admiring the neat rows of plants and vines, well cultivated.

"My goodness," said the preacher beaming. "You and the Lord certainly have done a wonderful work here."

"Yea, I guess," said the farmer, "but you should have seen it when He had it by Himself."

# 11 Run, Don't Walk

The dogs are in a tizzy—I am putting on my boots. This final, certain sign that we are going out signals the approaching acme of their lives. Never mind that we do this every day, twice; each renewal of the Great Adventure is fresh, and cause for rejoicing.

They have been watching for the signs, alerted by the internal clock that tells them: <u>Stand By</u>! My movements have been monitored, each sound screened for prewalk preparations. Animals have acute powers of anticipation. Mary noticed that when she was getting ready to go somewhere Smiling Sam couldn't go along, he'd slump into a corner and sulk. She studied her routine to learn how he knew. Simple—when going out alone she put on lipstick and Sam picked up the soft sound of her opening, then closing the drawer where she kept it. A fellow once told of sneaking up to the second floor of his house, while his dog was in the basement, and in a faint whisper spelling out W-A-L-K. In seconds the dog was at his side, leash in its mouth, eyes asparkle, tail fanning .

It's That Time! Dogs that were mopish are enfused with robust health. Hard sleepers are roused and ready. Now comes the warmup routine: stretching and dropping to forepaws in the ready-to-play position, rushes to the door and back, tail flexing, exchanges of nosings, vocalizing.

Boots on, I am ready; more celebration. All three crowd through the bottleneck of the door and spill out into the yard. At the end of the driveway Sandy turns on Amigo, growling in mock anger for that remnant of her challenge to Amigo's top-dog position. A weak challenge, ignored by Amigo, then Sandy saves face by running to take the lead.

George tears down the hill to the riverside park, feeling so good he does his midair whirlaround–a gymnastic diversion he picked up in his days as a free-lance stray. He runs, leaps up and flips around full circle before landing. He does it, as near as I can tell, just because it's fun.

They race away in different directions, surging with freedom and energy, pausing occasionally to see if another has turned up something of interest. They'll run rampageously for the first half mile or so and then close in by me, exuberance spent. Now they are manageable, orderly—Amigo on the point, Sandy just behind me, George far to the rear, because beagles have more stops to make.

The river is blackboard gray this morning, rippled in silver by a slight wind that makes it appear to be flowing upstream. When you live by water, you fall into noticing the condition of the stream first thing because each day brings a difference, differences that somehow foretell the day's temper.

The air has a bite to it and I wish I had worn gloves, but the chill will pass as the blood begins to move in me and by the time we return, my jacket will seem too much for this day.

The walking of dogs is an enterprise to be undertaken conscientiously. I speak here of bona fide walks, perhaps better described as runs or hikes, not those dart-out, dash-back-in flights for the sole purpose of letting a dog do his business. Nor those once-around-the-block excursions that only tease an animal but allow the lazy master to quickly regain the comfort of the couch for two, three, four more hours of tv, complacent in the belief that he has performed his duty to the dog.

Such shirking arises because people presume that taking the dog out is strictly for the dog's benefit. Walking a dog does the walker as much, probably more good than the dog. It is forced exposure to the outdoors, being in it and of it, not driving through or looking out the living-room window. How can one appreciate the warmth of home without ever feeling frozen, or know the blessing of air conditioning unless in relief from the hanging heat?

Exposure to every element of weather fortifies against colds, nature's air cleanses the lungs, rain encourages running for cover, snow requires leg exercise. Excess calories burn. The infectious cheer of the dog enhances one's mental health and the canine drainage system teaches discipline by the regularity of demands.

Such a shared health program takes planning and preparation. Time must be set aside. My twice-daily outings total about two hours because we cover 5 to 10 miles. Unthinkable? That's probably half the hours I've been cleaved to television, flipping channels and grousing about nothing good on.

Proper attire, appropriate to the season, is basic. Practical clothes are de rigueur; designer stuff is out. Jeans sturdy enough to withstand the scrapings of brush if you take to the woods. Waterproof boots with gripping soles are needed three quarters of the year, for snow, rain, mud and early-morning dew. A cap or hooded garment to ward off sudden rain showers and insects dropping from trees. Serviceable jackets for varied weather—with lots of pockets.

I need pockets because I go fully equipped. Provender sustains endurance for the long haul; I take fruit in the morning and raw vegetables in the evening. Munching on carrots, radishes, celery, potato slices, peppers and so on spoils the appetite for that huge fattening meal you think you're entitled to afterwards. I carry a supply of oatmeal cookies, not for myself, of course, but because the dogs enjoy a snack along the way. Strays we meet and fenced-in neighbors we call on become sociable over cookies.

I often take along a tape recorder or a notebook. Dazzling insights that come at any moment must be recorded; thus I am working while walking. The recorder also enlivens the trip with music, although I am not one of those umbilically dependent upon a boom box, ear phones, or car stereo for life. Still, the soaring resonance of a violin concerto or coloratura aria is thrilling beside a creek among tall trees.

Setting out, one needs to shed the confining skin of human culture, let it fall open to the way of nature and wildlife. This is a subtle milieu to which humans have become estranged and need a deliberate act of attention to catch the small surprises, wonder and unreckoned tragedies.

We come upon a runoff pond below Bennett's Landing and Amigo running ahead unknowingly flushes a big bird which thrashes from the trees edging the water and rises right above me. It is so close I hear the long wings beating and make out that it is, Yes! a blue heron! Crooked neck, long beak, legs tucked under and trailing, silvery blue, just as the bird book describes.

Its wings work powerfully as it climbs and gathers speed, soaring over the trees on the riverbank, then swoops low over the gray water, pumping and wheeling smoothly and as it departs, calls out: Aaaaaaaaaawk. AAAAAAwk! A raucous, godawful racket, so unbecoming such a graceful creature.

The dogs are oblivious to the heron's flight. They are prowling through the underbrush, hoping for a rabbit. This is one of our most frequented sites, a couple of miles along the river bank from home. We pass the city's campground and dump, the Fulton Boat Club and a field for tobacco, end up among the wet-season bogs and sparse woods around the dock where Dee Bennett keeps his towboats and the barges they pull in for cleaning and repair. Dee actually wants us there, figures our passing through on evenings and weekends when nobody is around is like having a free watchman; one hot Sunday afternoon I alerted him to a brush fire that threatened to burn out of control.

Finding places to run dogs takes some exploring, and going where you have never been before brings forth curiosity and bravado. You cannot be intimidated by No Trespassing signs, automatically erected by property owners to establish dominion. Nine times out of ten they can be ignored; the tenth being those enforced by shotgun. The trick is to establish ingress and egress, venturing through a few times until you are accepted, even greeted, as a fait accompli. Behind those No Trespassing signs I have chatted up property owners eager for talk. In one field we often traverse, the owner keeps our path mowed down and ignores the rest. We sometimes climb the ridge above the Hillside Inn; happening on the manager one day I told him we were the Critter Patrol, there to protect his customers from such beastly threats as coon, possum, rabbits and snakes. He studied me a moment, then withdrew in silence. Now he waves hello whenever I see him.

A suitable site ought to be away from all traffic possible, give room to roam, offer high snooping potential for seen or unseen residents of the wild, and have water at least in puddles for thirsty dogs to drink and flop in to cool off on hot days.

Golf courses are top flight, off season or on dismal days when only the hardy play. Following the out-of-bounds stakes leads us around the outer limits of the course, lined by woods into which the dogs can plunge.

Golf courses provide a bonus: lost golf balls. I've picked up hundreds more than I can use so I scrub them up and sell them to the country-club pro as part of my recycling program. Interesting socioeconomic phenomenon: the most expensive golf balls are to be found on Sunrise, the public course frequented by the laboring class, while the cheapies are lost at the country club, where the affluent play.

Several different venues are advisable; I have eight or ten to chose from, depending on mood and circumstances. Some are tougher, like climbing a ridge, or inaccessible during high water or crowded with humans in summer. Variety is necessary to avoid boredom; mine, not the dogs. They are creatures of habit who quickly pick up the customary routes and thrive on familiarity. One afternoon I decided, just for a change, to go around the golf course in the opposite direction. The dogs were baffled. They'd run away then stop, turn and look at me to see if I was really serious about this strange departure. They had lost their groove. I never tried that again.

Cemeteries are good for running dogs. We have a special reason for going to Springdale; Amigo's former owner is buried there. She meant so much to him that her profile is engraved on his tombstone, a reasonable likeness. We visit the grave and pay our respects.

I never noticed the clouds darkening but here it comes—a downpour of cold, slashing rain! The dogs don't have to be called when I run for cover. Nearest is a picnic shelter a quarter mile away. We run right into the slanting torrent, coming down so hard the drops pound my jacket. Amigo and Sandy are loping by my heels, their ears beaten down, fur drenched and flat. George is far back, holding out, coming tentatively.

Under the shelter, we wait for George and for the rain to stop. It doesn't look like it will so the procedure now is a series of wild dashes from one cover to another, underneath a bridge, the roof overhang of a building. A pointless procedure. We get just as soaked as if we hadn't stopped.

We reach home, relieved. Much shaking and moisture sprayed around. I go for the towels and they line up to be rubbed off. The exhilaration of our flight begins to subside. They will eat ravenously and sleep well tonight. So will I.

# The Third Book of George

Mrs. McCoy is out this morning, cleaning up the flood plain in front of her place as usual, burning off brush and disposing of refuse. She keeps on working when I stop to chat, as usual. We remark on the mildness of the day, how the high water hasn't been as high this spring but the jetsam is as plentiful as ever, the four Northern Pintails that wintered over, and other matters of consequence.

Mrs. McCoy is a diminutive widow woman of who knows how many years, for whom hard work is as quotidian as breakfast. She and her late husband settled on this bottomland long ago and farmed, lived frugally and acquired land piece by piece until now she owns most of the riverfront on the Kentucky side that we reconnoiter.

She keeps the flatland almost lawnlike, much of it mowed by a young niece of local basketball fame who can wheel a tractor around as if she were born to it. I asked Mrs. McCoy one time why she didn't farm the land any more. "Not enough money in it," she said, "make more out of campers."

Each summer she and a nephew who owns a section of the bottoms pull in dozens of mobile homes to rent to city folk who want to trade the heat of Indianapolis and Cincinnati for what seems like a cooler climate by the water. Her most bountiful harvest comes during Fourth of July week when the Madison

Regatta gives hundreds of people an excuse to throw up a tent on a marked-off scrap of land where they can party, party, party and occasionally watch the races. This free-fall of profit is a matter of some chagrin to the volunteers of Madison across the river who work year round to plan, arrange, finance and stage the weeklong activities and gain little or no return from Mrs. McCoy's financial farming.

She lives alone in the original farmhouse, surrounded by unused barns and outbuildings, all white. She once kept a dog for protection but he was killed by a car passing on the road in front. Late-night revelers coming along that road sometimes turn into her drive, frightening her. So she keeps a double-barreled shotgun by her bed and when she's awakened by intruders, she goes to the window, drops the sash from the top and fires off two shells into the air. An inexpensive, effective security system.

We are well known on this side of the river, especially to the canine residents. We park in the lot at the boat ramp alongside pickups with empty boat trailers, their owners already on the river. We pass under the rumble and clank of vehicles on the bridge overhead and follow a narrow low-water strand of sand at the water's edge that runs a mile and a half downstream before a promontory of steep rock prevents further progress.

Across the field of the plain above, a tiny terrier named Spike comes charging at us from a big white house of lovely symmetrical design with a border of noisy kids. If one of my dogs bothers to move toward Spike, he beats it back to the protection of the kids.

Further on, two hounds tied up at a trailer house across Coopers Bottom Road complain about our intrusion, not too angrily because our coming breaks their boredom. Along in here we are joined by Jesse, a fat brown pooch of questionable origin and friendly disposition. Jesse will join our exploring party but hang close to me waiting for the cookie break, follow to our turnaround point and then back to see us off at the parking lot.

Each trip turns up some minor marvel—a shucked snake-skin, the annual invasion of mayflies, a fisherwoman pulling in a large-mouth bass and a good-sized bluegill in a span of ten minutes with no excitement whatever.

One hot afternoon I sighted what looked like a huge bird high above the river that loomed closer and grew bigger and became a fellow in a hang glider who descended to a slow, grace-ful landing in the open field almost beside me. He was down from Indianapolis, draw here because the updrafts formed by the hills and valley of the river make ideal gliding conditions.

As we drew near the bridge on the way back I stopped to watch a pickup basketball game on an outdoor court in a field. A young man, older than the other players, left the game to come over and talk to me. He had seen me come by before and had always admired my beagle.

George had finished investigating the grassy clumps around the pier supports of the bridge, moved toward us prowling the high weeds lining the boat ramp. "He's sure a husky one," the young man observed. "Make a fine sire." He explained that he has two beagle pups at his farm, bitches he wants to breed. Said he plans to train them to hunt so they can lead their pups to learn, if he can get a litter. I think how George never was trained to hunt, picked it up on his own and suffers the errors of the self-educated.

The fellow, said they call him Rick for Richard, is sweaty from the game but would rather talk beagles than play basket-ball. He lives with his wife and mother-in-law, who "love the dogs," on 40 acres more or less out in the county. Rick spins a vision of a heaven for beagles out there.

The thought comes to me—the ideal place for George. He needs room to roam and on a farm he wouldn't be getting him and me into so much trouble. His romantic yearnings certainly qualify him for breeding and would make an honest dog of him. And he really isn't my dog; he's a stray who came and hung around.

By the time Rick put the question: "I don't suppose you would part with him, would you?" I was considering that it would be almost unfair to deny George this chance. Afraid I might change my mind, I offered my beagle to the stranger, who was immensely pleased. I called George; he came to me more obediently than usual. I picked him up and handed him to the fellow, and said only, "Be good to him."

Driving home across the bridge, the front seat beside me was very empty. Regret struck me first with alarm and then with a sinking helplessness. "It's the best thing for George," I said to Amigo and Sandy, "he'll really like it there." I repeated it to myself.

When I drove into the carport and opened the door, George was not the first one out. Our return was the same except that one of us was missing.

I had done the right thing, placing George where he belongs. Ended his hardscrabble existence as a stray and his brushes with the gas chamber. Still, for days I had to fight my selfish emotions; I missed him. His absence was undeniable; one less bone to pass out, no whine at the door, one dog short at bed check.

My mind played tricks to cover his loss. I absently called for him when it was time for a run. I still bought food for three. One night, I dreamed him back, afraid in the dream I was only dreaming.

I am weak, I suppose, but the vision of George cavorting in beagle heaven broke down. I wanted him back even if it wasn't the best for him.

But I had handed him over to a stranger almost without a trace. I had a name but no phone, no address. Rick had said he worked for Charlie Bolton at the River Terminal in Madison. I went by there and inquired. A woman in the office said Rick only worked there off and on; they hadn't seen him in months. "He's got a girl friend around here somewhere; he might be with her," she said. The image of the proprietor of beagle heaven was becoming tarnished.

I inquired at the Kentucky Souvenir Shop where I buy my lottery tickets because Bob Rowlett knows everybody. He gave me the name of Rick's mother-in-law, who lives in a mobile home on some road out in the county. Route 3 would get it.

I wrote an in-care-of letter identifying myself as "the fellow who gave you the male beagle" and admitted I had made a mistake, described how much I missed George, told of my past history with him, how the other dogs missed him, how giving George away had broken up our family. If sentiment wouldn't move him, I offered a proposition: another male beagle would do him just as well; I'd get him one or pay him the $25 going rate for beagles. I even offered George's stud services when his dogs were ready. I included my phone number.

For a week I waited, no call. George was resourceful; he might escape. We took a run every day on the Kentucky side to make our presence known in case George might be around looking for us. During walks on our side, I kept looking across the river to the boat ramp that was our meeting place, sometimes almost thought I saw him.

I wrote another letter on the chance that he didn't get my first one. Again I offered to pay, this time "whatever you think it would cost to get a male beagle like him." I badmouthed George, noted that I didn't know how old he was but that "you would probably be better off with a younger dog." I pointed out that George had been doing things his way all his life and was pretty set now and it would be a lot easier to train a younger dog. I remembered to tell him to call me collect.

No response. People along our route had begun to notice George's absence. "Where's the beagle?" they would ask. It was difficult to give a plausible answer. One morning I made the attempt with a retired gentleman who moves his mobile home into the city's campground every spring and spends the summer. He'd watched us go by for several seasons now and missed George.

He listened intently to my tale of folly, then chuckled and said, "Mister, you got yourself taken by a dog trader."

I'd been told of a beagle farm over in Kentucky that sold or rented hounds to hunters for the season. The place was said to be always in the market for beagles, no questions asked about where they came from.

I had little to go on except this: dog traders are in it for the money.

I wrote another letter, a brief one, offering $100 to get George back.

The very next morning when Amigo and Sandy sounded off at a car pulling into the driveway, I went to the door to see Rick opening the car door for George, who ran out dragging a line of rope.

The guy caught the rope and untied George, who scurried around sniffing Amigo and Sandy.

The beagle breeder, erstwhile dog trader was all smiles, silly smiles. I said little, pulled out my wallet and handed him the $100. He smiled some more, got in his car and left.

George gave me a quick wiggley greeting when I went to him. Then he checked out the yard, the water dish, the carport, the garbage cans. He was home.

# 12 The Latest Poop

Of all the perceived threats to the common good—drugs, crime, pollution, the national debt, violence on tv, bureaucracy, even taxes—none so radicalizes a segment of the populace as the specter of a solitary dog dropping a temporary deposit of biodegradable nutrient on the impoverished environment.

To ward off such a calamity otherwise sensible citizens resort to poisons, traps, and guns, make demands upon overworked police, write letters to Ann Landers, and press public officials to adopt pooper-scooper measures.

Such zealots pressured the aldermen of a nearby city to pass something called the Sanitary Disposal of Animal Feces Required Ordinance. In the years it has been in effect not a single case has come to court but copies of the ordinance are bought by the aversionists to sneak into the mailboxes of nearby dog owners.

The situation creates such anomalies as New York City, where residents make sport of wading through heaps of uncollected garbage on sidewalks and streets, but where a pooper-scooper law is strictly enforced.

Now, right here in Historic Madison, members of the City Council have caved in to a cranky minority and adopted a pooper-scooper ordinance that fixes an unsparing $1,000 fine on offenders, thus demonstrating that our public servants can be tough on crime.

Dog owners themselves are having to put up with a lot of crap. Moreover, the rights of 54 million canine Americans are being abrogated. A full airing of the issue is long overdue.

Investigation reveals three underlying causes for this mess: the Perfect Lawn Syndrome, Property Creep and Outhouse Phobia. A case study will be useful to show how these causes interact.

A neighbor of mine, whom we shall call Fred, is an outwardly decent sort, a retired merchant of some means, a fine house and a lovely wife we'll call Molly. They make a handsome couple setting off on their early morning walk or dressed to the nines for an evening of cocktails and dinner.

Fred is restive in retirement. Slowed somewhat by a heart condition and missing the stimulation of deal-cutting, he plays a good game of golf with his cronies at the country club, takes occasional fishing trips up north (where the most exciting catch is a wild card to fill an inside straight), reads Louis L'Amour westerns, goes to church regularly and puts out corn for the squirrels in his trees.

This is not enough to quell the managerial juices still flowing in his veins. Fred is always pushing some project: goading the other directors at his bank to take on more investment property, pressing the tenant on his farm for higher tobacco yields, worrying over how to put his vacant real estate to work. Around home, few months pass without a renovation—blacktopping the driveway, resetting the roses, adding an overhang to the carport—which Fred oversees with a watchful eye.

Each morning without fail, like a patroon surveying his manorial estate, Fred inspects every square foot of his lawn to ascertain if the lawn-care firm he employs has missed a swath, and to search for any foreign object that might blemish the manicured grass. This is where I run afoul of the Perfect Lawn

Syndrome.

If Fred's inspection turns up any dog doo, he nabs me. It matters not whether Fred has observed the offense; the presence of poop not there before is prima facie evidence that one of my dogs is the culprit.

I'll give Fred this much: He confronts me; he doesn't call the law. That's his good-neighbor policy. Even if I believe my dogs have been falsely accused, after stalling for a time to preserve my pride, I go over and clean it up, muttering expletives. That's my good-neighbor policy.

I've never had the temerity to handle it the way Hank does. Hank is an Indianapolis lawyer who keeps a summer apartment here, plays golf and cards with Fred, and walks his white toy poodle a lot to sneak a cigarette because his wife won't let him smoke in the house. Hank will stand right there in the yard chatting with Fred while the poodle does his business on the unsullied turf and then laugh and tell Fred, "I'll send you a bill for fertilizer in the morning."

Fred gets up at the crack of dawn and goes to bed with the chickens, as they say, so I presume he has rural beginnings. It doesn't matter. Practically everybody in Indiana claims to have come from the farm; it is where they get their conservative values, like stubborn resistance to taxes, liberals, and outsiders, roughly in that order. One of the traumas which can mark farm-bred folk for generations is the Outhouse Phobia.

Bear with me here, because this gets messy. In the good old days down on the farm, there was no indoor plumbing. There was the outhouse, situated (understandably) at some distance from the house: a quaint little shack, a one- or two-holer depending on the size and affluence of the family, with crescent apertures for aesthetic decoration and ventilation, furnished with Monky Ward catalogs for reading and sanitation.

Most farms kept a flock of poultry—chickens, ducks, geese, guinea hens, turkeys—which roamed free, scratching the yard bare and leaving layers of residue everywhere. For humans, a trip to the outhouse was a wade. Lanterns were necessary for night visits.

It was deeper in the barnyard, where livestock left thick plops so unforgettable that today they are sentimentalized in contests at fairs to see who can throw "cow chips" the farthest. Every farm had a manure pile just outside the barn which grew from mucking out the stables. Farmhands all wore boots. Manure was saved as a valuable commodity, then as now a natural, cheap fertilizer.

Few advances were greeted more heartily by farm folk than septic tanks and generators to pump water, and later, rural electrification. These blessings brought human ablutions inside, the luxury of baths in something besides wash tubs, and eliminated those slippery trips to the outhouse.

It follows that the squeamish horror of living and walking during that primitive era has never been fully exorcized in some unfortunate souls, but lies dormant in the unconscious and surfaces in shock at the sight of dog doo. Perhaps these people deserve our sympathy, at least the organization of support groups and a hot line to call when the affliction manifests itself.

Owning a home of one's own is the American dream, but it comes at a price; it is the psychic one that concerns us here. Owning a piece of property can turn a warm, caring, peace-loving citizen into a terrorist in the cause of property rights. No nation defends its borders with more zeal than homeowners hereabouts guard their property lines. Some take on a fortress mentality, enclosing their abodes with fences. I've often thought there's a fortune to be made constructing moats for property owners, surrounding their holdings with water trenches, perhaps stocked with piranhas, and a drawbridge with gingerbread trim.

It takes only a minor property-line incident to touch off hostilities. Leaves from the trees next door blow over on her property, kids cut across his yard on the way to school, a neighbor's cat violates her flower bed.

A woman down the street regards an unwary animal walking across her yard as an invasion roughly equivalent to D-Day. She puts out poison-baited traps that have killed the pet cats of an impaired little boy across the street and all the squirrels in the block. She's affronted by the counter-complaint that her kids bounce balls and throw rocks at other people's houses. This is characteristic of property compulsives; they are clear-eyed to infringements of their property rights, but blind to the rights of others.

Other defenses are No Trespassing signs and classified ads in the paper that threaten unspeakable consequences to any who dare set foot on posted property. These are necessary because trespassing is not a crime—not even a misdemeanor—only a tort requiring civil action for enforcement, a fine source of revenue for small-town lawyers.

Chronic property compulsion leads to the contraindication known as Property Creep, a form of hallucination in which the subject attempts to protect imagined as well as real property. The concept of "ownzone" from the empirical literature is helpful in understanding the manifestations of Property Creep. Affected persons presume they "own" everything that falls within proximity of themselves or their property; whatever concerns them in any way is their "ownzone." Property Creep leads an owner to assume that the public street and sidewalk in front of his house and the alley to the side or out back is within his ownzone. Some time ago, residents of two adjacent houses in the next block got into a furious fight over claims that the other was parking on the street too much in his ownzone. One day one went out, got into his truck and rammed the other's car. They fought it out in court, each dismayed that the judge failed to uphold the concept of ownzone and instead assessed damages for the wreckage.

Our big event every Fourth of July week is the Madison Regatta, which draws thousands of visitors to the unlimited hydroplane races on the river. The only place out-of-towners can park is on streets near the river. Each year, locals place chairs, boxes, cans, and other obstructions on the street in front of their houses to prevent the invaders from parking in their ownzones. They can be heard defending this practice saying, "I live here all year long," that is, ownzone rights have been established.

Ownzones attach to the zoneowner and thus are portable. One year, some of our Property Creepers went down to the riverbank a few days before the outsiders arrived for the Regatta and established ownzone rights to the best viewing places. They staked out and roped off large blocks of ground, covered them with plastic tarpaulins and put up No Trespassing or Keep Off signs. Even public officals wondered at this and banned such practice as harmful to the grass.

Property Creepers are everywhere: i.e., the motorist who claims the entire road for some distance ahead, behind and on both sides, tailgates behind as you drive up the entrance ramp, roars around at his first opportunity, disgusted that you have dawdled in his ownzone.

On any Sunday in church, a Creeper may approach unwary individuals seated in what had been an empty pew and announce with a glower, "I _always_ sit here." Creepers declare ownzones of seats on the bus, picnic tables in the park, curb space in front for parades, even—although this lacks scientific certainty—the emotional ownzone described as "my space."

Returning to our case study, one can grasp how these phenomena commingle in an unsuspecting citizen. We noted how Fred carefully tended and inspected his close-cropped holdings, searching out the dreaded dog doo—manifestations of both the Perfect Lawn Syndrome and the Outhouse Phobia. Fred's addiction to Property Creep is manifested in his ongoing insistence that a neighbor whose house stands between Fred's and the river should cut down all trees, vines and other appurtenances that might obstruct Fred's view from his dining room window. Too frugal to buy a place right on the river, Fred declares, not always successfully, that a space of open visual access through the property of others is his ownzone.

The Perfect Lawn Syndrome, Property Creep and the Outhouse Phobia are loosely founded in fact, but grow and thrive on misinterpretation.

Take the Perfect Lawn Syndrome. Lawns are an American phenomenon, traceable to Pierre L'Enfant, the planner who laid out Washington, D.C. He eschewed the fenced-in front gardens of Britain and the European tradition of buildings abutting streets. Instead he sought to symbolize the freedom of democracy with long reaches of open space from dwelling to street and unencumbered vistas along frontages for blocks.

Thus to every village and hamlet came lawns, which we Americans regard as the formal presentation of our property to which we devote much loving care and money. A neighbor who lets his lawn go untended is disdained as slovenly, if not unAmerican.

Only in America are grass plants not permitted to achieve maturity, but are cut short like botanical castrati to preserve their tender beauty. Our drive to produce a grass carpet is counterproductive. In the minor case, at least three inches of growth is necessary to shade out crabgrass; in the major case, the Perfect Lawn Syndrome is destructive to the environment. Botanist Gerould Wilhelm of the Morton, Illinois Arboretum says that mowing grass "to within inches of its life" results in as much water runoff as pavement. The runoff carries top soil and the noxious chemicals we pour on lawns into sewers and streams, destroying aquatic life, lowering the water table, and creating droughts.

The sanctity we attach to property rests upon a cloudy rec-ollection of Holy Writ. Somewhere in the Bible, it is vaguely recalled, God told man to subdue the earth and have dominion over it, a proof text for property rights.

God did, indeed, so instruct man—the man was Adam, the time was the sixth day of Creation, and the property was the Garden of Eden, according to the account in Genesis. As the Creator and Original Owner, God imposed one deed restric-tion—that neither Adam nor his mate Eve should eat of a certain tree.

In an era when computer literacy exceeds Biblical literacy, our recall of that first real estate transfer may be faulty. Adam blew the deal; he listened to Eve, who listened to the serpent who tempted her, and they ate the forbidden fruit of the restricted tree. God not only canceled their property rights but evicted them, dispatching Adam with "Cursed is the ground because of you. You are dust and to dust you shall return."

As feisty an exponent of protecting nature as Kentucky poet and author Wendell Berry has said that a close reading of Scripture shows "we humans do not own the world or any part of it…in Biblical terms, the 'landowner' is the guest and steward of God."

This is closer to the earth view of the American Indians, who believed not that the land belonged to them but that they belonged to the land. It was from the Indians that we stole the land we now guard so fiercely. One of the Hoosier legislature's first acts of statehood was to order the Indians out, off their land, keeping their name for the state.

Thus we have seen that the furor over dog droppings rests on slippery ground. One could argue that the guardians of prop-erty rights and their Creeper brethren are themselves guilty of receiving and possessing stolen property. Adherents of the

Perfect Lawn undermine their very goal with practices that are inimitable to nature.

I do not wish to be unreasonable. I stand ready to abide by the principle that those who are responsible for making a mess should clean it up. My resolve would be reinforced if others would do the same. If those responsible for the plastic jugs, fast-food containers, beer cans, old tires, broken bottles, and other unbiodegradable detritus that my dogs and I encounter every day on the riverbank will clean up their mess. If the poop chasers in government would crack down on the power plant on the west end of town that burns the cheapest, dirtiest coal and spews black toxics from its stacks 24 hours a day seven days a week. If the lawn lovers would put emission caps on their power mowers and weed cutters—and the same for boaters on the river whose motors leave a sheen of oil on the water.

I need more than nasty warnings and the threat of a stiff fine. If those who muck up the environment me and my dogs live in would stop contaminating our ownzone, I'd turn into a zealot in the cause of canine cleanliness. I'd even get a pooper scooper.

# 13 Does He Bite?

We are out on our beat, visiting with the canine neighbors and testing each block's alarm system. Sandy is ahead on the sidewalk sashaying along in her fashion-model swagger when a sedan full of family pulls up to the curb, doors fling open, and kids disembark from every portal.

A two-year-old toddler clutching a stuffed doll waddles straight for Sandy, shrieking with glee, "Mean doggie! Mean

\* Guest illustration by Bruce Bolinger

doggie!"

She throws a plump arm over Sandy's back and hugs, cooing, "Mean doggie."

Sandy accepts this greeting as she always does, with a nose sniff and tail wag. Sandy is kid-friendly, takes pummeling or petting with unending patience; the most any child has to fear is a wet lick. When my granddaughter Sara was too small to climb up on the couch by herself she could make it by using Sandy as a footstool, stepping on her and climbing over and up. Sandy hardly noticed.

A young woman with a baby on her hip walks up on the hugging in time to hear her daughter's greeting. Somewhat embarrassed by my presence and Sandy's forbearance, she says, "He's not a mean doggie."

As we resume our walk the mother herds her brood toward their door and I can hear her explaining, or trying to.

That young mother was coping with the dilemma facing any conscientious parent: how to warn your child about a mean dog without turning the child against all dogs. The toddler got the message all right, repeated the "mean" part and lovingly acted out the "doggie" part.

Kids are drawn to dogs like plants to the sun. When we pass near the small fry swinging and climbing in the riverfront park, the first one to spy us screams "Doggie!" to alert others, who take up the chorus. They abandon the apparatus and come on the run, a few slowed momentarily by a shout from a distant adult "Don't you go near those dogs!" They swarm to us, then hesitate and ask, "Does he bite?"

The question is so predictable I can't resist. "Of course. How do you expect him to eat?" or sometimes "He's a police dog; he eats a policeman every day." My lame humor is lost on them but they take my tone as reassurance and proceed to the petting that pets are meant to receive.

We draw a crowd because children are dog curious. "What's

his name?" "What kind of a dog is that?" "Is he a boy or a girl?" Then, while the dogs submit patiently to gentle, awkward strokes, they tell me of their dogs, invariably creatures of unusual character. A lad down the block noted for telling whoppers has a handsome Husky at home and he told me straight-faced that the dog's father was a grizzly bear.

Once introduced, youngsters unfailingly call my dogs by name, and never miss a one. Streaking by the house on their bikes, they hurl out: "Hi Amigo. Hi George. Hi Sandy." Amigo is visited regularly by a shy lass who waits on her bike at the end of the drive until Amigo comes out to meet her for some secretive girl-dog talk.

When my troop is moving in close order down the walk and we come upon a parent and child, if the tyke wades into the pack I volunteer "They won't bite" to calm the apprehensive parent. My dogs are friendly, which I attribute to freedom from excessive restraint that relaxes them and kind treatment from humans that socializes them.

They have been tested. Some tots rush at a dog and grab it as if it were one of their toys, and just as disposable. A boy advanced menacingly on Sandy thrashing his arms out yelling "Shew! Get away!" obviously imitating some adult. A teenager throwing rocks into the river saw George wading in to cool off and began slinging stones at him. The act was so callous I blew up and lectured the thrower in language I don't often use. Some bullies like to chase a dog and make it run away, just to show how tough they are.

Adults are more furtive. Sauntering down an alley some distance behind the dogs I observe a man up ahead who sees one of them, growls "Git!" and flings out a foot. Then he notices me and hurries silently by. A woman who keeps vigil over a city parking lot from her front door always snarls "Shew" at the dogs before I appear, oblivious to how witchlike she looks. On warm evenings a neighbor sits out on his driveway and shouts "Git away!" at dogs trotting by, even across the street.

Despite these provocations, my dogs have never responded in kind; they run away from an aggressor. I won't tolerate a vicious dog or one that bites. If one of mine should bite someone, he would undergo severe corrective training and if he did not respond, I'd have that dog put down.

Some dogs <u>will</u> bite and sad to say most often they bite children, probably because kids are around dogs more. It happens to boys more than girls. They are not usually bitten by strays, but by their own or a neighbor's animal. It is also children who are most often the victims in fatal attacks.

There are no reliable figures on the annual number of dog bites; the Humane Society of the United States estimates somewhere between one to three million. The total is declining but the number of serious bites appears to be increasing, probably because of more ownership of large dogs bought for protection and security.

In 1990, at least 24 deaths caused by dogs were recorded, the most in recent years. Every death is a tragedy, but that number is miniscule compared to the number of children and adults killed every year by guns or motor vehicles.

The "mad-dog" menace is largely legend. Rabies in canines is negligible; cats are more often infected because they are not commonly inoculated.

Media reports on the dog-bite problem tend toward the sensational, cite unreliable statistics, quote obscure experts and recklessly use the term "epidemic." In the end, the dog-bite problem is a problem of humans.

The pit-bull controversy is an example. Fatalities inflicted by the breed have brought measures to outlaw pit bulls. Said one animal control officer, "If there were no pit bulls, then people who want a dog that has a certain kind of reputation—Rottweilers, German shepherds, Dobermans—would simply get something else, treat it the same way, and similar tragedies would occur." Some breeds are aggressive, bred to be so by humans to fill the demand of security-minded householders who want a guard dog, the meaner the better.

Not too long ago dogs were bred to fight each other to the death, wildly cheered on by spectators who bet on the outcome. Though illegal, like cock fights, this recreation continues in secret. Aggression is American sport.

Dogs have no control over the reputations they acquire. The same German shepherd breed trained as an attack dog can become a rescue dog that saves human lives, detects illegal drugs or guides the blind or disabled.

Some common sense rules can avoid dog bites. Don't approach an unfamiliar dog, especially one that is tied up or confined. Let the animal see and sniff you first before petting. Stand still; don't run past a dog. If it appears threatening, avoid eye contact and don't scream. Back away slowly. Whether the young mother can convey all this to her two-year-old is another matter.

"There are no bad dogs, only bad dog owners" is one of those comments full of both truth and futility. Owners can reduce the bite risk. Spaying or neutering an animal helps; a dog that hasn't been fixed is three times more likely to bite. Confinement should allow the dog room to run, in a fenced yard not on a chain. Chained animals tend to be more aggressive. In most states owners can be held liable for any injury or damage caused by their animals providing the injured party did not contribute to the attack by provoking the dog, ignoring beware-the-dog warning signs, or trespassing on the animal's territory.

One set of trespassers with expert experience on the "does-he-bite? question are tradespeople who make daily incursions into canine territory—letter carriers, delivery drivers, meter readers, and such. All have tales of their encounters. One of their conclusions: it is the dog that an owner assures them "won't bite" that nips them in the end.

Most of these stalwart servants accept the condition that

dogs go with the territory and make the best of it. One morning on the putting green I eavesdropped on two Federal Express drivers topping each other with dog-bite stories, each episode gaining in hilarity and laugh-off relief.

Express drivers appear to take a wade-right-in approach that dogs seem to respect. My UPS guy has taken the trouble to ask my dogs' names and even though he calls them all Amigo, that disarms them.

The single mother who reads our gas meter and fears not making ends meet more than dogs apprised me that dog owners are marked; listed for each address in the meter book are the canines to be expected. Mine reads: two German shepherds. In fairness to George, I told her to add one beagle.

The protest that dogs on duty put up over some invasions of their property seem eminently logical. Exterminators bring a foul-smelling spray that would drive off any human, let alone a smell-sensitive pooch. Mowers of lawns push noisy, fearful vehicles around. Garbage collectors raise a frightening racket with the roar and beeps of the truck, yelling and clanging down can lids.

I've noticed that newspaper carriers, if adult, draw the ire of dogs, but a boy or girl delivering the paper provokes much less fuss. Don't send a man to do a boy's job.

Candidates for political office who come soliciting get my vote if the dogs like them, as reliable a judgment as their stand on taxes.

The sorriest of the lot among dog-space invaders are those who should have resolved the does-he-bite? matter long ago— letter carriers. Throughout history, the mailman and dog have been adversaries, celebrated in story, cartoon and calendar art. The mailman ventured forth unafraid, turned his foe into friend where possible; where not, he wore his nips and scratches like a badge of courage.

Alas, no more. The Postal Service has gone soft, turned into a league of whiners. My mailman can serve as an example of how the gumption of letter carriers has declined exponentially with the increased price of stamps. Chuck is a burly veteran of the carrier corps, proud father, officer in his union, avid Cincinnati Reds fan who listened to games on his Walkman as he covered his route. He knew his patrons by name, not car-sort or occupant, and they awaited him despite the bills he brought. He's now retired, has covered the 75,000 miles a carrier lugged that bag in the time of his 30-year service. Moreover, he has survived the canine menace, despite an inordinate aversion to dogs.

Chuck let me know early on I was to keep the dogs inside when he came around. The advent of mail delivery was a time for roll-taking and lockup. If I forgot, maybe out in the yard planting petunias with the dogs dozing nearby, from far down the street he'd shout, "Get the dogs inside!"

The most the dogs ever did was bark, from a distance, and not even that after they got used to him unless he startled them by emerging suddenly around the corner of the house. It got so they'd hardly even look up; Chuck had become part of their habitat. But once I got a call from the Post Office with a not-very serious request to keep the dogs away; they were aware of Chuck's phobia.

A fellow in the next block has a small border collie named Samantha, kept in a fenced-in yard, who barks at passersby as much in greeting as warning. At Chuck's insistence, the householder was required to erect a rural-type box atop the fence gate, so Chuck could stuff in the mail from the sidewalk, saving himself the walk up to the porch.

It was reported to me that Chuck wouldn't deliver to one resident who had a mail slot in her front door. He was afraid her dogs would bite him through the slot.

Ultimately, Chuck achieved a kind of bullied rapprochement with my brood. One afternoon Sandy was out in the yard poking into a bush when he arrived. He startled her and she barked in surprise. "Shaddup," he growled. Sandy cowered, her feelings hurt.

The Postal Service has become so sensitive it has joined up with the Humane Society of the United States to sponsor National Dog Bite Prevention Week, an all-points campaign including cards to postal customers instructing them on How To Avoid Being Bitten and How To Be A Responsible Dog Owner. I appreciate the Post Office's concern for my well being and its help in educating me, and I am not one of those who regularly makes light of postal problems. However, I note with some per-plexity that it is always the customer who is held accountable for solving the problem of dog bites.

Why, I venture to ask, does the Postal Service hire people with a neurotic fear of dogs and assign them to deliver mail? Couldn't such phobics be screened out on job application or interview, or at least assigned to duty behind the counter? Does the Postal Service offer its carriers any training on How To Be A Responsible Carrier In Dog Territory?

In the latter years of Chuck's service, I noticed that on rainy days he came around in a little red car with the Postal Service shield on the side. Good, I thought, why should he have to walk in the rain? Then he began driving on nice, sunshiney days. After Chuck retired, all carriers were furnished new white Postal Service trucks for a complicated drive-park-walk coverage of their routes.

Surely this extension of motorized routes to the city in some way must increase efficiency and I would not deny postal carri-ers shelter from the elements, But for years it has been the faith-ful, intrepid letter carrier we thought was portrayed by those oft-misquoted lines of Herodotus: "Not snow, nor rain, nor heat, nor night keeps them from accomplishing their appointed courses with all speed."

No more. Postalpersons driving around in comfort may be efficient. But not heroic.

# 14 To Sleep, Perchance

The weight pressing down on my chest rouses me from deep sleep to the beginning of consciousness. When the capacity for thought comes, I know without opening my eyes that he's there, but I stall, conjure the deliciousness of sleep and the futile hope that I can ignore him.

He makes no sound, hardly moves, waiting. I feel his paws pinning me to his demand that I wake. Slowly I open my eyes and see the nose and nostrils, oversize so close to my face, and the intent eyes behind.

In the half light—it must not be 5 o'clock yet—I make out the long ears and the slant of his body.

I know he won't move until I speak to him. "My god, George, don't you know what time it is?" realizing immediately how ridiculous that sounds. I get a small tail wave of recognition.

"Oh, all right." I reach for the covers and throw them off of me and over him, a ritual he relishes because it means he has won again.

As I slide out of bed he emerges from under the blankets, jumps to the floor and follows me to the door. I let him out and watch while he heads down the sidewalk, off on his morning rounds and another busy day.

Back in bed, the thought occurs to me: "I wonder if anybody else in the world wakes up in the morning with a beagle standing on his chest staring down at him?"

One thing dogs do exceedingly well—arguably their fore-most achievement—is sleep. They devote long hours to the practice of it, 15 to 17 hours a day if given the chance. And they don't just sleep, they work at it, assiduously striving to improve their performance.

They don't simply lie down and go to sleep, a complicated rigmarole must be followed. First, various locations must be scouted to find one suitable for sleep, with a corner or wall for back support, proper air circulation, and if possible, an over-hanging table or drapes for cover. Some dogs are escapists who slump in stairwells and behind furniture. Some are hangers-on who don't want to miss anything, even in sleep; they choose a well-trafficked doorway or a place on the kitchen floor behind the mistress of the house when she is cooking dinner. For sleep-ing outside, a separate set of criteria obtains. The effect of sun-shine, shade or streetlights must be considered, the spongy characteristics of grass and leaves, the precise flow of breeze over concrete, and again, depending upon the pooch, either a place of privacy under bushes or an observation post offering purview of all that goes on.

Once chosen, the site must be sniffed for the aroma of pre-vious occupants or contamination from dog deodorants or flea spray. If bedding is present, it must be rearranged according to an ancient canon known only to canines. If no bedding is present, the carpet or bare floor must be thoroughly scraped to assure that it is immovable. Should the site's foundation be agreeable dirt, preferably in a flower bed, this shall be burrowed to appropriate depth, texture, and temperature.

Myth has it that dogs turn around seven times before they lower themselves for slumber. As with all myths, this is true only if one believes it. A careful count will disclose how erratic the turning process actually is—sometimes several turns, sometimes none at all. Instinct's purpose here is to fit the body into the place prepared for sleep, whatever it takes.

Furthermore, the raison d'etre of this folderol is to disassoci-ate the sleeping site from human arrangements. So how silly it is for dog fanciers to put out those expensive basket beds or fluffy pillows.

This is not to say that a sleepy mutt won't, first chance he gets, invade human sleeping quarters—appropriate your bed, your couch, your most comfortable chair. But note that, once there, he sets about transforming whatever is moveable to his own requirements.

Whoever first raised the specter of "things that go bump in the night" most certainly had a dog. When humans speak of a "sound sleep," they usually refer to a long night of uninterrupted rest. Dogs will have none of that. Who hasn't been awakened in the middle of the night by a resounding thump, and when the frightened mind clears, realize that it was only Rover flopping down into a new position?

Dogs sleep under a quota system which requires them to occupy a certain number of different places per night. I don't know what that rate is but I have observed that Amigo, George and Sandy will settle for the night in their chosen places and in the morning, they are in those same places. But all night long I am aware of a mass movement from the thumpings of feet on the stairs, the tic-tic-tic of toenails on bare floors, many floppings down, like a mongrel game of musical chairs. If I should rouse in the middle of the night and turn on a light, I see that they have traded places. But by morning they will be back at their assigned posts, having completed their quota of moves.

Another insight gained from watching dogs sleep is proof positive that Bowser has a brain. Let anyone who thinks not observe the animal in throes of a dream—body lurching, legs jerking, wimpers that are barks stifled by sleep—Bowser is unmistakably dreaming of a chase. Dreams rely on memory; memory requires a mind; ergo, dogs have intelligence.

As to the matter of whether they possess a reliable alarm mechanism, I am less certain. Mr. Hays across the street swears that his cat wakes him at exactly 5 o'clock every morning. My dogs may approach me on the subject of getting up, peer at me in bed at unscheduled times and finding me uninterested, return for 40 winks themselves.

Now please, let's keep this next part to ourselves, because it concerns a matter of some delicacy—people letting dogs sleep with them, in their beds. As you know, certain fastidious folk regard this practice as disgusting, childish and unhealthy. The same folk who sleep in twin beds or separate rooms from their spouses and regard any display of affection, even among humans, as frivolous and likely to spread germs.

The sanction for dogs sleeping with people is limited. Hollywood, from which we receive many of our values, has decreed that dogs are welcome in the beds of small boys. How touching the scene of Jimmy snuggled up to Pal, ruffling his ears as they drift off to dreamland. Perfectly within the limits of family values.

Although I can't know, I suspect that a number of adults allow Patches to jump up on the bed and spend the night there. I do know one couple who split up and claimed that the dog came between them, in bed, but doubtless there were other problems as well.

So, unless you have a Great Dane, I say, why not? A warm body is a warm body.

I really could not say otherwise, because George sleeps with me; well, in truth, I sleep with him.

It is purely a question of squatter's rights. He naps on my bed as is his wont, in the cozy, dignified curl position. Which reminds me that I have been meaning to have a talk with Sandy about some of the positions she assumes, especially while on the couch beside me—flat on her back, legs akimbo, most unladylike.

George takes possession of our bed early, while I am still glued to the tube. When I come to bed he is lying right in the middle, soundly snoozing—although this may be an act he puts on for effect. The problem is on which side should I crawl in to disturb him the least. Once I do, no matter how unobtrusively, he stirs and groans and communicates his displeasure. I settle as comfortably as the room he has left me will allow. But his chagrin seems to mount until after about 10 minutes, when I am close to dozing off, he gets up and leaves, stepping on me and over me in a transparent expression of contempt.

Some time later, when I am asleep, he is overcome either by forgiveness or yearning for the softness of the bed, and I feel a sudden pounce and some walking around while he selects his space. He knows I know his druthers so he pauses tolerantly until I assume the position. It's a stance like running in bed, on my side, legs stretched in a stride. George then lies hard against the back leg—sometimes the front; it varies.

He's set for the night but after a while I ache for a change. If he is cocooned on my knee, I can barely move. Usually, I manage to slip a leg out and leave him there and go back to sleep. During the night there is some sleep-dulled groping until we find— Praises Be—that best-of-all sleeping states: warm back to warm back.

James Herriot begins one of his books with the hardly deniable opinion "that there are few pleasures in this world to compare with snuggling up to a nice woman when you are half frozen." What can I say? A dog is certainly no surrogate for the warm body of a woman on a cold night, or any other for that matter. But waste not, want not. A dog will do as a substitute until...

Besides, beagles are cuddly and George loves affection. He has discovered that when I'm lying on the couch dozing or watching television with one arm hanging over the edge he fits ideally under my hand for an effortless delirium of backscratching. He can sleep happily with my hand on the back of his head, fingers fitted perfectly under his ears. Even his scent is not offensive; pungent and distinctive, though I grant you, not as appealing as a woman's.

In the wee hours of the morning when duty calls and George does his stand-up routine to awaken me, and after I have let him out and have gone back to bed, I miss him. I really do.

# 15 Name Game

When a man has lived the biblical four score years and ten with a name like Ora he develops a pesky conviction that every living creature is entitled to a name that fits. I feel empathy for canines forced to endure life as Cutie Pie, Poochie, Honey, Crank or Grunt, collies called Lassie, a boxer named Buttons, any bulldog stuck with Pug and dogs labeled Brownie, Blackie, Blue, Inky, Ebony, Ochre or Pumpkin—color coded or not.

Dogs deserve better. They can't express their views on the matter (any more than misnamed babies) but I have it on human authority—Andrew Rowan, director of Tufts University's Center for Animals and Public Policy—that naming an animal is not to be taken lightly. "Give your dog a bad name," he says, "and get a bad dog."

When endowed with godlike authority to afix an identification to a living being we humans sometimes get clever or silly. We chose names to suit us more than them. A Civil War buff commissions a puppy General Lee or Beauregard, the student of mythology goes for Thor or Zeus, the literati come up with Ernest or Zelda. We memorialize old lovers and immortalize celebrities, living or dead. Lately there's been a run on Star Trek characters. The guard dog becomes Danger or Fury. A naturally exuberant puppy may go through life as Bonkers or Dizzy, a gift pup as Valentine or Yule. Leave naming to the kids and you get

Cuddles, Barney, Benji or Lassie.

Some namings are indeed clever. A newspaper editor named a beagle Adlai after twice-beaten presidential candidate Adlai Stevenson because the pup just loved to run. My son had a beagle who disappeared for days of travel over the countryside. Her appropriate name: Gulliver.

Cats come in for some inventive titles, usually with a feminine lilt, although many remain Kitty all their lives, except for Kitty Kitty when called. A music lover over on Main Street named her three cats Beethoven, Mozart and Mendelsohn. Some historical license was taken here; Beethoven—the cat—is nearly blind, not deaf. An elderly cousin of mine has a handsome black cat she calls O.B., short for Obediah;, the prophet of Queen Jezebel's time who defied her and saved 100 prophets from execution. "I think it is a good name for a cat who does as he pleases and is fed and loved by me," she says.

The only restrictions on naming dogs are for registration with kennel clubs—no duplicates, limited number of letters, nothing presumptuous or unbecoming. The rules resemble those for naming thoroughbred horses although horse names, while wacky, are much less pretentious and seldom require an aka designation in news reports. Ch. Altana's Mystique, a German shepherd best-of-show superstar, is also known as Steeker. Ch. Salilyn's Condor, a happy English springer spaniel who wows the crowds and trots off with honors, is known to his friends as Robert.

Advice from the experts is simple and sensible. Names that end in a vowel—Friskie, Tina, Bingo—are said to be more recognizable. Two syllables are best for callability. Ro-ver carries farther than Spot; if you have to yell Here before Spot you might as well name him Here Spot.

If you name a pet something like Flo or Joe and then have to shout No! to halt some misbehavior, what the animal hears is poetic but confusing. Several pets in the house without different sounding names makes for mixups.

To the counsel of experts I would add my preferences. A pet's name ought to have livability; it has to last a lifetime. Think of people who hate their names because what was so sweet for a baby turned sour over the years. Feisty might not be when he grows up. Boney may put on weight. Puddles will learn to go outside. Crank's disposition may sweeten with age. I knew a beagle named Sox for white paws that grew to a no-sox brown.

In this day of concern for self esteem, why add misery to the life of a blameless animal with names like Ugly, Silly Willie and Dumb Dog? Why not lift the pooch up with a challenge? If he's meak and shy, call him Tiger or Spike. If she's ugly or awkward, flatter her with Venus or Pretty. Small mutts shouldn't be constantly reminded of their stature with terms like Tiny or Junior. A dog needs help from his support system.

Sometimes appearance and/or characteristics are unreliable for picking a name. In the next block lives a Lhasa apso who looks her name—Cupcake. But when we go by she comes tearing out after us in unCupcake fury. Still, she has delivered 10 litters of puppies as sweet as her name. Next door is a white miniature poodle named Snowflake who does not descend quietly when she wets the grass, but proclaims her presence to the entire neighborhood.

As to following my own advice on dogs I've named, Tag was a good choice because he never quit tagging along. Penny, a Dalmatian, was a family consensus and fit her nicely. Amigo, Sandy and George came prenamed.

A friend asked me to name her newly acquired dog-pound refugee, a who-knows-what breed with zest for play and mischief. I decided on Zacharias, because I've always favored biblical names. He didn't much match the character but Zak for short fit his zippy quality.

Most of my namings have come with strays who follow us

home or drop in and stick around until I can find them a permanent situation. Boomer, a border collielike mutt, had a delayed fuse on an booming personality. I was rather pleased with Bart, a black Benji type with the verve of a Black Bart pirate. I placed him with a dog-happy family across the river in Milton and he often joins us when we take the Kentucky air.

Our daily rounds visiting the neighbors offer a somewhat longitudinal study of the fitness of dog names. My sample is limited to perhaps half the dogs we encounter, the ones to whom I have been formally introduced or overheard being called, and whose names have not slipped through my leaky memory.

By my hunch, at least one in three households has a dog, some more than one. Cats are more numerous but harder to count, more secretive, sitting in windows or hiding under automobiles. They emerge in force at night, wail their peevish love calls or dash across streets defying dogs to give chase. Cats also abide in clusters, several to a household. A lady on Central Avenue has more than even she may have counted. I've seen one in four different windows of her house, with a couple more outside.

My animal-population survey suggests that pet owners are underrepresented in the councils of government, which sometimes adopt restrictive animal-control measures at the behest of a handful of cantankerous complainers. If pet people—citizens, taxpayers and voters all—ever got together they could yank some political leashes themselves.

Cathy and Axel are only nominally restrained by a four-foot fence around a yard in the next block. Cathy is a tan, mixed-breed so anxious for company that she frequently leaps the fence and joins us for our walks. If her folks are at home when we pass on the way back, she dutifully jumps back into the yard. If her humans are gone for the weekend, she sometimes spends a day or two with us. Cathy's name seems to fit her sociability; I sometimes call her Catherine, which brings the same face-licking response as Cathy. Axel is an opposite, a big, black German shepherd trained in disaster rescue. He's kept mostly in a sealed pen in the back, but his deep no-nonsense bark is enough to scare away any intruder. Axel is a good name for an obedient animal with a sense of duty.

We encounter a number of German shepherds, whose names and dispositions attest to the varied temperaments of the breed. Max, short for Maximilian, is a quiet, dignified dog who shares a yard with a noisy cocker, whose name I never caught. A military man a couple blocks down the street favors shepherds and exotic names like Moonbeam and Loki, which say little about their serious but well-behaved demeanor. Molly was the timid companion of a towboat pilot. She was so secure prowling the decks of the towboat that she became unwary and was killed crossing a street. Ozzie is my candidate for the friendliest dog in town, a husky tan-white shepherd who jumps up on the fence to greet us and wiggles with such glee that he drops his cookie.

For friendly, Ozzie has competition from Gretchen, a chocolate Lab whose mistress says "She is almost too friendly." Topped out with a red bandanna around her neck, she could have a career as an official greeter. Another chocolate Lab, Sadie, has a penchant for wandering off and getting lost, always seems torn between the temptation and fear of taking off.

Of course, names can be deceiving. Daisy is a Doberman pinscher with the job description of junkyard dog and a bark and behavior to match. She is staked in the center of her owner's junk-piled backyard, only partially enclosed by fence, where she snarls and growls and carries on a fierce altercation with Sandy—as long as the fence separates them.

One day as we were passing, my dogs up ahead in the alley, Daisy accidentally slipped her tether. She charged around the fence and started after my dogs. Suddenly she stopped, looked around and came slinking back. She cowered behind me, looking lost, until I led her back into her yard and refastened her tether. Then she crawled into her doghouse and hid. Off of her junkyard turf, Daisy acted like a daisy.

Dogs can have split temperaments, one on their home territory and another off. Rocky is a sizeable shaggy black mutt whose yardmate is a tiny beagle named Honniker. Fine name for a beagle, a breed that often seems to perform like an adult dog in a puppy's body. Rocky lives up to his name, ferociously barking and jumping at the fence every time we pass. One day to his surprise he found himself over the fence, out of his yard. He ventured only a short way toward George, only half Rocky's size, then groveled on his back in the submissive-puppy position. George sniffed him, decided he was all bark and bluster, and trotted off.

The most aptly named dog is Trouble, a mean, nondescript mongrel who threatens or attacks my dogs whenever we are within a block of his place. Dogs are not fools and soon I found they were going around that block, avoiding Trouble.

Among ill-fitting names are Bandit, an exuberant little cuss who goes into a conniption of joy and excitement at our every appearance, and Babe, a black Labrador of such strength and enthusiasm that she can knock me down jumping up in greeting.

Some dog names reveal the owner's lack of imagination or caring. Akita is an Akita whose master couldn't get beyond the breed name. Poochie is a lonely pooch staked out at the Fulton Boat Club whose neglect equals his sluffed-off name. Midnight was an anything-but-black dog whose namer must have thought it cute. Grown animals with no more name than Pup or Dog have lazy masters.

The Morgans live in a stately mansion on Broadway with neatly landscaped yard surrounded by a four-foot wrought-iron fence. They keep dogs, English setters inside, and outside a magnificent Alaskan husky called Star. We visit Star on night walks, find her waiting at the corner of the fence. Then begins our cookie-break ritual: those on the sidewalk get a piece of oatmeal cookie and Star gets hers. Then we walk a way, Star following along inside the fence, pause for another round of cookies, and so on until my supply is gone. Star is mannerly, even ladylike, in accepting her portion, but if I ever pass that way and forget to bring cookies, Star glares and noisily bawls me out. The name Star fits her grandeur, but she could just as appropriately be called Cookie Monster.

On one of our visits to Springdale Cemetery, to roam and pay our respects to Amigo's original owner buried there, we met a man with a beagle puppy, six weeks old and full of rambunctious joy. George went off chasing rabbit scents and Sandy chased after George and Amigo was left to half play, half fend off the puppy's invitations to romp.

The man was a weathered sort, muscular arms tan against his undershirt, an odd-job worker I'd seen around and one who had recently tasted the fruit of the vine. I asked him what he called the puppy. "Ann," he said and thereby hung a tale, which he told.

He was hanging around the house one day with the woman he lived with when he ran out of beer. He asked her to go out and get him some. She refused. He <u>told</u> her to get him some beer. She still refused. Now a man without his beer can become desperate and he got mad. He <u>ordered</u> her to get him some beer. She got just as mad, walked over to a corner, picked up his shot gun and, not expecting it to be loaded, aimed at him and pulled the trigger.

He lifted his undershirt and lowered his pants to show me an ugly, three-way, 10-inch scar, still mean looking. "Cost me $18,000 to get my guts put back and sewn together," he said, rather proudly. "Wasn't her fault," he added suddenly, "she didn't know it was loaded."

The woman's name is Ann—and now it is the puppy's.

Now that's true love.

# The Fourth Book of George

The call was confusing. The woman at the minimarket wanted to know if George was all right. The last she saw him he was headed down the alley for home and she just wondered how badly he had been hurt.

Hurt? What happened?

He was hit by a car, chasing a cat across Harrison Street, the busy one that leads to the bridge. He got up and started home, so she figured he might not be hurt too bad. That must have been an hour ago.

My God. No, he hasn't come home yet.

I barely thanked her for calling before I put down the phone.

I rushed out to the alley and ran-walked down the block to Harrison. No sign of him.

Oh no. Could he have gotten a little way and crawled off in the bushes and died? I fought down fear of the worst. George was tough. But where is he? I called and whistled, startled at my own sound in the empty alley.

Twice I searched the block between Harrison street and home, peering into yards, looking under bushes. I poked into every possible place of concealment close to home. No George.

Guilt was getting to me; I shouldn't have let him run around on his own. But he wouldn't have it any other way. Whenever we got back from a run, the other dogs would go inside. George would stand out at the end of the driveway, pondering whether to come in or not. Usually he did; you could almost tell when he reached his decision.

Come on George, where are you? I visualized him turning up suddenly. My mouth was dry from whistling and I was getting hoarse. The thought of him hidden somewhere, suffering, made me frantic. Wait. I've got to be more thorough or I could pass right by him. I began a search pattern to cover all the streets and alleys for three blocks and the park down the hill.

Nothing, not a trace. If I used the car, I could cover more territory, so I ran back, got the car and drove, slowly, looking from side to side. George knew the car; maybe he'd come out or whine if he saw it. I asked kids I came across if they'd seen George; none had. They looked concerned at first, then went back to their play.

If he had died...where somebody had seen the body, it might

have been reported to police or the dog pound. I could call to find out, but I didn't want to face that. Maybe later.

What would Mary think? When George first started hanging around she'd said she wasn't partial to beagles, but she paid for his shots out of her animal welfare fund. One Christmas when I left town with Amigo to visit the kids for the holiday, just overnight, I let Mary know I was leaving George out. He'd be fine; I left food outside and he could sleep in the dog house as usual. The temperature dropped to 19 that night. George had been out in much worse, but Mary got worried. She couldn't coax him into her house so she went over and relined the dog house with paper and stuffed in more straw. Then she took over her electric heating pad and an extension cord! But she couldn't find a plug close enough to stretch to the dog house.

I parked the car and wandered out into the alley; not searching now, thinking, about calling to see if George...if a beagle dog. . .if the body of a beagle dog.. .had been found. I guess I'll have to. As I turned to head for the house, I heard a whine. And there he was! Walking slowly to me, wagging his tail.

George!

I bent to hug him, then realized he'd be hurting. I stroked his warm head and told him how worried I'd been. He whimpered weakly, glad and relieved. Squatting there in the alley, I checked him over, gently feeling his legs and body. He was trembling and winced at my touch. I could find no breaks, not even any blood. But he was in pain. As carefully as I could, I picked him up and carried him home.

As soon as I saw Mary's car pull into her driveway, I called her. Mary knew what to do with injured animals. She didn't even volunteer to check him over, but called the vet, who luckily was still in. We left immediately, Mary driving, me and George in the back seat.

He was silent, snuggled in my arms, shivering. He didn't

move; he seemed to fell safe now. Tough, independent, fearless George—now just a scared little dog. He was that way during thunderstorms—his only fear. He'd come to me as if I could do something about the terrifying sound, and I'd put him beside me on the couch and sooth and stroke and talk to him until the storm abated. He'd whimper if I stopped before the storm did.

The doctor's examination found nothing visibly wrong except for some dirtied, flattened fur on his left shoulder. George winced when the vet pointed to the mark. He gave George a shot for shock, said he wanted to keep him overnight and take x-rays the next day.

The x-rays showed George had a broken bone in his shoulder. They also revealed some of George's past struggle for survival—scar tissue on a rear leg that had been broken and apparently healed by itself. And several pellets of buckshot, still embedded in his body.

Treatment required immobilizing the limb to give the shoulder break time to mend. Thick brown bandage was wrapped around his neck and shoulder, fastening his left leg up against his chest. When I picked him up at the vet's, George looked pathetic at first, then kind of funny. He didn't seem to mind; his concern was to get out of there and back home.

Those next three weeks with a three-legged animal, I was immobilized. The first few days I kept him confined to the house and yard, which wasn't difficult because he couldn't move fast enough to sneak out the door and couldn't leap up on the roof of the doghouse and onto the patio to escape the backyard. When I shut him in and took Amigo and Sandy out, I felt like the warden of old movies who slammed the cell door shut on the falsely convicted prisoner. When we returned, George was as hearty as ever in greeting Sandy and Amigo, but he pointedly ignored me.

His gait across the bare floor and the rhythm of his sound

changed from a busy tic-tic-tic to a lumbering tic-flop, tic-flop. He ate like a horse, though, which had to help him heal. He couldn't make it up the stairs to sleep-watch while I was working in the study, but he came to me when I sat on the couch to watch tv and allowed me to lift him up to nestle against my leg and sleep contentedly. He remained there all night after I went to bed.

When George knew it was time for us to go out, he took up a position right by the door, waiting. I finally gave in and let him go along, hopping happily, slowly, but getting there. The first trip or two, we shortened our walk and even Amigo and Sandy seemed to understand why. Then George made it clear that he didn't want to turn back, and the walks lengthened.

Each day we went farther. George stuck close to me, or me to him; still, he found scents of interest and places to investigate near our route. We'd rest at the turn-back point before returning. As he mastered the three-legged gait, he assumed this was the way it was always to be, so he tried returning to business as usual—poking into places that need poking into, giving chase when a rabbit appeared, standing on three legs in the river, looking a bit foolish, but cooling off.

Trouble was, he'd run out of gas. At a fairly far piece from home, he had given his all. He didn't complain; he just stood there, unable to go any further. Rest didn't restore him, so I started carrying him home.

A 30-pound beagle can weigh 900 after lugging him a while. The delicacy of the hold required to avoid putting pressure on his wound made it harder. We soon agreed upon the proper grasp and he was sympathetic to my labor. I had to stop and rest several times to regain circulation in my arms before we got home.

I devised a scheme. By now, I had figured about how far George could go before he gave out, so before taking the dogs out, I drove the car and parked it as close to the give-out point as I could. Then I walked back home and we all went out for our trek. When we came to Exhaustion Point, we all piled in the car and drove home.

I was happier than George when the day came for us to go to the vet's and have the bandage removed. The only noticeable change was that his body under the bandage stank and his fur was cleaner there than the rest of him. The doctor gingerly worked the atrophied leg, cleaned him up and pronounced him healed.

The vet said it would probably take a week for George to regain full use of the leg. It took him two days.

# 16 Sacred Cars

Coming back with the dogs from an evening prowling the woods upriver from Bennett's Landing. Sandy and I walking down the county road into town, single file, her in front. Our half of the road has been freshly blacktopped with a quick-dry asphalt surface that shines new next to the gray opposite lane, now four inches lower. Yellow and black paving vehicles stand waiting in a field to finish the job. The project seems cosmetic; the old surface looks smooth enough and this road carries little traffic.

A cream-colored car looms ahead in the distance, coming in our lane. Sandy is poking down a dog-wide line on the outside edge of the road. There's no shoulder, only a shallow ditch alongside. I follow behind, watching the approaching car, make out two people in the front seat. The vehicle isn't slowing down or giving way for us as most do. It's holding to the new surface, coming straight at us. I think to grab Sandy and lunge for the ditch but too late, the car is upon us. I cringe as it whips by, glimpse a middle-aged woman driving, staring straight ahead. My pants leg flutters in the draft as the vehicle passes inches away; from the side window an older woman peers out, eyes wide and fearful. We aren't hurt but I am furious. I turn and yell after the car, shake my fist in the air, swear incoherently, so tight with rage I can't find the vile words I need.

The car recedes with unslackened speed, still on the smooth new lane, closer to the outside than the middle.

My anger crowds out the fright I should feel. Sandy saunters ahead, unconcerned.

I've had worse. Twice while jogging on the shoulder I've been forced to dive for the ditch by drivers who intentionally aimed their cars at me, then turned away laughing as I leaped for my life. Each time my menacers were young males proving their mettle. I can imagine the rallying cry: "Let's scare the hell out of that old bastard."

One afternoon I was jogging about 10 feet off Vaughn Drive on a long expanse of pavement where motorists pull off to view the river. Two automobiles approached in the traffic lane. No threat until suddenly the car behind veered off the street onto the lookout shoulder, speeded up to go around the other one. I was caught between as the two passed on either side. Once around, the errant driver swung back onto the road and roared away.

At the very same place a few weeks later I was spectator to a terrifying case of deja vu. Two young women were walking toward me on the lookout, one pushing a child in a stroller, when a car pulled off the road onto the lookout to pass another one. The women and child were engulfed from behind by the cars passing them on each side. They weren't aware of the danger until it had passed. They seemed more surprised than alarmed. Not me; I was trembling.

Such scary episodes are nothing new to nondrivers who share the road with drivers. Walkers, joggers, bike riders all have their own horror stories of near rundowns, usually concluding, "Drivers think they own the road."

The woman who nearly ran down Sandy and me may have been a fine person, not driving. When she sighted us in her lane she must have quickly calculated the circumstances: the interference we posed, the convenience of the smooth new surface, the uncomfortable bump down the four-inch drop if she turned into the un-repaved lane. All but automatically she chose her convenience and comfort over the threat to a mere pedestrian and a dog.

Any person afoot with human body weight and an ounce of logic is foolish to go near a rolling ton of metal, plastic and glass with killing power that increases by velocity. In a contest between human and machine over the same thoroughfare, might makes right. If the two should collide and calamity result, the unvoiced reaction of driver to victim is apt to be: You had no business being there. To which the defeated victim might rightly respond: Why not?

In an astonishing number of places designated for public passage, access is provided for motorists and denied those not driving. Sidewalks are lacking where the public is expected, even encouraged, to visit, or laid down like an afterthought unsafely alongside streets because right-of-way space was used up for vehicular traffic. Crosswalks are often missing at stop streets as if pedestrians aren't worth the paint. Tax money goes for the needs of the driving public; the nondriving public gets what's left. Officials have been known to grumble about having to spend money to make curb ramps for handicapped persons, money that could have been used to repair potholes.

The domination of the motor vehicle over almost all else in our national life has been gradual but is virtually total. We have become a society which worships wheels, bowing before the graven image of the sacred car.

Our subjugation may have begun when the first noisy horse-less carriages scared horsedrawn buggies and wagons off the roads. Those first motor cars—and a few quieter, slower electric cars—were luxuries only the few could afford so for a time horse and car comingled on dirt roads and streets. But not for long.

Moving under machine power was so thrilling, so fraught with status and perceived convenience that we were seduced.

The automobile was primarily a German invention, product of Daimler-Benz engineering, but some American devotees claim its conception. This deceit is prevelant here in Indiana, with good reason; the State Historical Society lists 522 different automobiles, trucks, motorcycles and cycle-cars made in Indiana, from Marmon and Maxwell to Stutz and Studebaker.

Indiana is car culture, home of the Indianapolis 500, the ultimate trial by speed and fury, and mecca to thousands of faithful pilgrims. A farmer with a fallow swell of acres can pave a racing oval and reap a bountiful harvest from Sunday afternoon midget-car races. Here is America's best-selling auto dealership: a father and son in Mishawaka who unloaded 96,478 Fords in 1993. Back-alley garages in any town can perform mechanical miracles, raise wornout clunkers from the grave, at little cost. At Buck and Don's, where my 74 Chevy is repeatedly rejuvenated, I've never heard talk about anything but cars and their symptoms, the ministering mechanics hovering over an ailing heap like specialists in consultation.

When men meet on the street here their greeting is likely, "Well, what are you drivin' these days?" and conversations among women at the laundromat often as not have to do with the model they've bought or want to.

Hoosier veneration of the automotive grows from the state's industrial history. It took Henry Ford to convert the rest of the country. By upping wages of his Detroit workers to a shocking $5 a day to mass manufacture a Model T they could afford to buy, he moved automobile ownership from dream to reality for working people everywhere. The spread of the gospel of wheels was collosal and continuous, to 140 million cars on the road today.

The number of vehicles on the road is increasing twice as

fast as the population. Miles driven have stretched a third in the last decade. The average commute to and from work has lengthened from 17 miles in 1983 to 22 miles in 1991, due to sprawling suburbs, where even more miles are rolled up getting from home to mall to Mom's and the orthodontist.

Only 5 per cent of us rides public transportation, and that's going down. Only 13 per cent car pool. We cling to the one-car, one-driver hangup like a nation of loners. Result: highway congestion costs $100 billion a year. We burn up 1.4 billion gallons of gas in gridlock, waste 1.2 billion hours stalled in our splendid isolation.

We pay mightily for transportation. In 1967 a new car cost 40 percent of an average household's income, today it swallows 50 percent. One car won't do; a car for every driver is almost the rule. Driveways of many a house or streets in front are clogged with sedans, a pickup or van and maybe a boat trailer, an investment in wheels as great or greater than the house.

Time was that owning a car was an adult prerogative; you bought a car when you could afford one. A generation ago the 16th birthday was a rite of passage when a teenager could get a driver's license and borrow the family car for a Saturday night date, provided some gas was put in it. In this motor age, youngsters barely out of day care race motorcross dirt bikes. Older kids compete on motorcycles, mopeds, go-karts and small dragsters. Pedal bikes are too tame.

The newsletter of my Audubon Society chapter recently asked in commenting on brown air: "Do you own a car, or does the car own you?" It's a pertinent question. How did we become so controlled by a piece of machinery?

It took years of conditioning. Advertising insinuated into our national psyche the double whammy that You Are What You Drive and Happiness Comes On Wheels. Snob appeal inferred that success is stepping up to the luxury model. In the ad fantasyland, drivers are attractive and happy, all roads are empty of traffic, and parking is always available at the front entrance of your destination. Hollywood's ever-present car chases and explosive crashes turn speed and danger into make-believe entertainment, inuring us against accidents ever happening to us, until, of course, one does.

We are sold chargers that can accelerate from 0 to 60 in 7 seconds as power we might need in a pinch. Market research learned how reluctant we are to leave our comfy cocoons and brought us drive-in, drive-through, drive-by convenience. Police never walk a beat, patrol only in their fortified cruisers. One wag suggested that the adjustable steering wheel was devised to get us in and out of the driver's seat around the girth we've acquired.

Here's a challenge: Next time you walk out your front door or drive to the store, pay attention to how much land is under asphalt or concrete. Building foundations, driveways, carports, sidewalks, streets, alleys, parking lots, ramps, courts, drive-in lanes, and runoff gulleys cover a good half of the good earth. In some cities you have to go to a park to see grass.

We are paving over America. Seventy percent of the land mass in Los Angeles County is paved over to serve vehicles. In other cities, it is 30 to 60 per cent. When an old building is torn down, no need to ask what for; it's to be a parking lot or parking garage. The Kentucky State Fair has 18,500 parking spaces, but 10 more acres are being purchased to add several thousand more. When nothing is going on the place is a concrete wasteland.

Our state representative sent out a newsletter to let us know how much state and federal money he'd brought into the district. Of the total, $8,776,000 was for transportation projects; $3,719,122 was for human needs.

One day soon we'll hear that the space shuttle is taking off for the moon with a concrete mixer in its cargo bay. NASA will tell us it needs to pave a landing pad, then hardstands for land rovers, then roads and parking for Moon Headquarters, warehouses and workshops, etc. By the time you and I get to go to the moon, half of it will be paved over.

We had a candidate for mayor who ran on a platform to widen Clifty Drive, our franchise corridor, from four lanes to six. He got elected, too. Of the two sure things in life—death and taxes—here in Hoosierland we fear taxes far more than death, but if a politician promises to cut three minutes off the time it takes to get to the video store, well, that's different.

Besides, only a small matching percentage comes out of "our" taxes; the rest is from the state and federal governments, which we gladly accept until election time when we raise ned with those tax-and-spend politicians in Washington and Indianapolis.

When local government can't shake money out of the capital, its service to the sacred car is limited to traffic control, safety and such, like setting a speed limit of 20 miles an hour on Vaughn Drive, our scenic riverfront road, and assuming it's being observed. A traffic survey that came to the attention of our Riverfront Development Committee found the average speed on the drive to be more than 30 miles an hour. We adopted a resolution urging three stops streets along the two-mile stretch, because pedestrians have a hard time trying to cross in peak hours. When we presented our recommendations to the chief of police he gave us 479 reasons why it would be unthinkable, impossible, out-of-the-question to delay drivers merely so people could cross the street. Even the mayor admitted he used the drive as a beltway to get around downtown without having to stop.

The most stirring example of blind municipal devotion to the sacred car has come downriver in Charlestown, a village with few parks and sidewalks where kids tend to play in the streets.

Motorists naturally resented this intrusion on their domain and a few cranky neighbors complained of the noise kids have been known to make while at play. So the Town Council adopted an ordinance that not only banished kids from streets but from the sidewalks as well. The measure prohibited children from "playing basketball, baseball, soccer, skateboarding, roller skating, hopscotch and all other games or activities in streets, alleys and on sidewalks, and in other public places where unnecessary noise disturbs surrounding residents." The mayor said a broad ordinance was needed so if a child was injured the city couldn't be held liable.

Charlestown's antiplay ordinance drew the ire of parents and brought embarrassing media attention. One national television commentator asked: "Who's in charge here?"

The Council's response was to lower the fine for a first offense from $100 to $10. Nothing was required of drivers to accommodate to the problem of Charlestowns' children with no place to play. At that point no child or parent had been arrested nor would police comment, a tribute to law enforcement officers, often a bulwark of sanity against silly legislation.

Upon reflection, where the Council went overbroad in its zeal to protect drivers from children was in banning hopscotch, an old-time, all-American family-values kind of kid game. I am gratified to report coming across several hopscotch grids scratched on the sidewalks of Madison. I can never make it past six or seven. My rock keeps missing the square I'm on.

# 17 The Thing Is...

Living with dogs is a learning and nonlearning experience. Some things you learn and some things you don't.

One thing I've learned is, if you're feeling grumpy and could use a laugh, feed part of your peanut butter and jelly sandwich to your dog.

\*\*\*

A thing I've never learned is: do dogs remember where they buried their bones?

***

Puddle water is preferred by canines over water in a dish because it is fortified with dirt minerals, has the bouquet of worms, insects and pollywogs, tastes fruity of leaves and twigs, and contains no chemicals.

***

Another thing: why do people put up so many bird houses for martins—multiple-hole mansions and three-story apartments—but I've never seen a house with a martin in it?

***

If you make a fool of yourself with a puppy, so will he.

***

Has Snoopy ever been on a leash?

***

Dogs are suckers for reverse psychology. They may turn up their noses at the scrumptious food you lay out, but if you hide it they will find it in no time. If you offer it to another pooch, they'll fight for it. If you can't get Duchess to go into a room, go in and close the door and see how soon she's scratching to get in.

***

Never get a white dog unless your carpets are white, your furniture is naugahyde, and you have an industrial-strength vacuum cleaner.

***

How do birds find a feeder, especially when it's under the eaves or hidden from sight in a tree?

***

Clutter in a house means: People Live Here. Clutter in an office means: Work Is Being Done Here. Clutter in a dog's place means: Occupant Asleep. Do Not Disturb.

***

Why does a hound who has been in the water always wait until he is up beside you to shake off?

***

The adjective "adorable" should be reserved exclusively for little girls in pretty dresses, and puppies.

***

Dogs have a sense of smell that is 250 times stronger than a human's, or 250,000, or 1,000,000, the experts tells us. Well, which is it?

***

Why do people who call the law to have a stray picked up, knowing full well there's a strong chance it will be destroyed, always insist, "I like dogs...?"

***

Dogs can be quietly expressive with their paws, lying non-chalantly in the head-up position with paws placed side by side perfectly parallel or one casually crossed over the other or one folded daintily under.

***

How do cats get away with it? There are more of them, they reproduce faster than dogs, carry rabies more, are more preda-tory, roam at night, screech and whine, get into vicious fights, dig up flower beds, scratch and bite their handlers. But nobody ever calls the law on them.

***

Humans take most of their liquids in the form of coffee or tea, soft drinks, juices, beer, wine and booze, soups and broths—rarely as water, straight. Maybe that's why so many fenced-in and tied-up dogs are so often or so long left without water.

***

Why does Rex wait until you are snuggled into warm and dreamy relaxation on the couch to decide he wants to go out?

***

What is it about the howl of a hound, so plaintive and

bawling, that strikes me as amusing?

\*\*\*

A ticking clock will comfort a new puppy, also does a lot to calm down a hurried human.

\*\*\*

If mayflies come to live their two days of existence and then die in late June or early July, why are they called mayflies?

\*\*\*

Mongrels are masters of nonverbal communication. They can charm with a look of innocent appeal, wag or wiggle for joy. They can sit and stare until you figure out what they want. They can deliver a gentle love bite. They can sulk in self pity or give you a gaze of disgust that makes you feel guilty even if you're not sure how you offended. They communicate caring beyond anything you deserve. All without uttering a word.

\*\*\*

The best bird feeder is the smooth table of the driveway. Spread some seed around and it's chow time! They feed in a frenzy with enough for all so spats are few except for doves; there's always a pair bickering. I know they mate for life but one is always getting after the other. Where did they get the reputation of billing and cooing like lovebirds?

\*\*\*

It may not be true that a watched plant never grows, but it sure grows slower.

\*\*\*

Why are Council members—Town, City or County—always concerned about animal control but never about animal welfare?

\*\*\*

A dog has as more gaits than a horse. He can walk, trot, run, gallop and lope like a horse's canter. He can also stride and amble—and bounce through brush like a deer, walk on narrow logs without falling off and step over obstacles without even looking.

\*\*\*

How can a pooch upstairs asleep hear the whispery sound of a foot slipping into a pants leg as an ear-splitting alarm waking him for walk time?

\*\*\*

Some folk who are stern and disapproving of the family pet will romp and play with her when nobody's around.

\*\*\*

When one sees a worm or bug on the sidewalk, why is it necessary to step on it?

\*\*\*

Dogs don't escape America's fixation on youth. The way business hires workers who are young, energetic and cheap and unloads them when they get older, want more money and draw benefits is like the pet owners who get a puppy that is small and cute and bouncy and when it grows bigger and older and needs attention drop it off out in the country or at the animal shelter to be put away.

\*\*\*

The thing is, how can they call it Pork and Beans when the can contains only a single piece of meat hardly as big as a bean?

# 18 The Dream Giver

If I hadn't been driving the steep curves of the road up Hanging Rock Hill I'd have wished it was snowing. In the ravine below the trees looked dark and lusterless and needed a fall of white, like I needed a lift from the dreaded trip to the laundromat. Across on the bluff side the sun's slant exposed rock yellowing and streaked wet brown, winter bleak.

On a straight stretch of incline a small red car was pulled off on the shoulder, empty, hood up signaling trouble. Bad place for car trouble. Poor devil. Soon there he was ahead, a tall man trudging along the roadside, carrying a dark object I supposed was a gas can.

I glanced in the rear-view mirror, saw the road behind was empty and pulled over in front of him. He came to the car and opened the door with obvious relief.

"Ran out of gas," he said apologetically as he settled in the seat and placed what looked like a portfolio in his lap. "I thought I could make it but I guess she just dried up."

"You'd have had a long walk," I said, visually calculating the distance to the nearest gas station.

"I need to make it to the Sirloin Stockade before 5," he answered, as if gas were of minor importance.

"Well, you still have time." I had planned to stop at Dr. Rimstidt's to get some Pet Tabs for the dogs and knew he closed at 5.

We introduced ourselves, shook hands awkwardly across the seat as I drove. "I'm an artist," he said and grasped the portfolio in his hands for emphasis. "I did a portrait for a woman who works up there and she gets off at 5." He opened the case to show me a pastel portrait of a pretty little girl, maybe five or six. Competently done, if that's how she looked. Cute, maybe flattering. Not too hard to do from a photograph.

He closed the case quickly as if shamed by his display of pride.

Apparently the guy needed to deliver his work and get paid before he could buy gas. "We'll get there," I told him.

He struck me as quite handsome, dark hair made distinguished by gray at the temples, eyes that seemed to flicker from bright to repose. His clothes were plain, worker type, long legs in jeans, rumpled jacket too thin for the day. He seemed restless. I told him I was a writer and knew what it was like to sweat out pay for a job, sometimes for months. He looked worried.

We discussed the uncertainties of our work. He'd been at his for 30 years. He'd done a book of portraits of past leaders of Ohio, where he came from. A New York publisher wanted to put it out but the artist couldn't come up with the money. They were really anxious to publish it, had lowered the downpayment but still he couldn't raise it. "That's not the way it's supposed to work," I told him. "They're supposed to pay you, You've got yourself in the hands of a vanity publisher."

As I described the workings of the vanity press I grew uncertain; instead of saving him, I was spoiling his dream.

When we pulled up outside the restaurant he got out, turned back and stood holding the open door, stuck for words. "I hope she's still there," I told him and he smiled, stepped back and closed the door very carefully, raised his hand in a two-finger salute, then hurried into the entrance.

Why I sat there I don't know. He's a grown man and when he gets his money should have no trouble buying gas; there are several stations among the businesses along Clifty Drive. Ought to be easy to bum a ride to his car. But I waited. Hell, it's Christmas time.

It was well after 5 when he came out, looked disconsolately right, then left, and saw me, brightened a bit and walked to the car. "Did she like it?" I asked as he crawled in. "Oh yeah, she liked it fine. She said her girl would be thrilled with it." He didn't seem gratified. "But she doesn't get paid until Friday and can't pay me until then."

This was Tuesday, I remembered, because I never go to the laundromat until after Monday washdays. "Did you leave the portrait?" I asked, knowing how people can forget about paying once they've got the goods. "Sure, why not?" he answered, flipping up a corner of the portfolio in resignation. "Well, let's get you some gas," I said and started the engine.

At the BP station across the highway I did the negotiating for a can of gas, no deposit; this is Madison not some big city. I paid and we started for the drive down the hill.

He didn't have much to say, nor did I, until we got to his car and he poured gas in the tank, remarked, "Have to save some to prime the carburetor." The little car started right off. He rolled down the window, thought for a minute, then, "I'd rather go down to Clyde's place and fill up. I can take the can back later."

For no reason I can think of I followed his car down the hill into the center of town to the filling station. As he drove up beside the pumps I followed. A young man in coveralls emerged from the station, walked toward the pumps, suddenly broke into laughter, flung his arms open and shouted, "Pee-cass-o!" They began an animated conversation, uninterrupted when the attendant pulled the hose from the pump and plunged it into the tank of the little red car.

He's known here, probably can charge the gas. But I told the young man to fill my tank, too, and when he finished I handed him my credit card and said, "Put both of them on that."

While we waited for the attendant to write the charge ticket the artist told me, "I live over there," pointed down the block across the street, "above Hinkle's." I knew the place. When I was a volunteer for Hospice I had a patient who lived there, upstairs over the all-hours eatery in a squalid furnished room.

"Hey, let me buy you a beer," the artist said cheerfully when I was signing the ticket. "No. I'll buy you one." He looked disappointed. "It's O.K." he said, "Harry at Sportman's lets me run a tab."

As we drove out the grinning attendant yelled, "See you, Pee-cass-o!"

The Sportsman's Bar on Main Street offers nourishment for soul and body to a blue-collar clientele. It is one of four similar establishments on a circuit around the block that is negotiated on Saturday nights by refugees from the farm, working stiffs, and rednecks from Kentucky who crowd the municipal parking lot with their pickups, secure there if the owners should be required to spend the night in the drunk tank. Their need of a sympathetic ear is fulfilled by a reliable corps of tart but understanding patronesses, and Harry.

Harry looks like a bartender. His girth is testimony to the quality and quantity of his stock. Rolled-up sleeves, apron wet from hand wiping, a man of few words who has heard it all but who busies himself emptying ash trays and clearing off empties while he hears it again.

"Hey, Artiste," Harry greeted my new friend as we mounted bar stools, automatically set a bottle of beer before him—Miller Lite. The artist motioned to the bar space in front of me and Harry served me the same, which I accepted although I don't like beer.

"So how's business?" Harry asked. The artist shrugged. "Plenty of business, not much money."

"Ho, Rembrandt!" someone shouted from deep in the back where four or five people sat around a table. "Come on back. We got something for you."

He looked to Harry, at me, then turned and sauntered down the long bar, which flashed from dark to color from blinking Christmas lights strung over the mirror and lined-up liquor bottles. He was greeted heartily with backslapping and smiles, soon settled into a chair at the table.

"They got him a subject," Harry said, observing the convivial gathering.

I sat silently, fingered the cold bottle, watched a small Santa Claus statue on the shelf behind Harry reach down into a plaster bag and jerk back up, slowly, down and up, down and up.

Finally I said to Harry, "What's his name? He told me but I forgot it; I've got a memory like a sieve."

"Paul. Paul Horster. Nobody calls him that. It's Rembrandt or Picasso or any other artist they've heard of."

Harry left to attend two customers at the far end of the bar and then to pass drinks to a fellow in a cowboy hat who came over from a table where he was sitting with a blonde in country western garb. Line dancers, probably.

The laughter from the table where Paul sat with his friends had settled down to conversation. Paul was sketching, his pad propped at one end on a bottle of beer gripped in his hand while the other moved on the drawing.

I was feeling left out when Harry wandered back my way, glanced with a frown at my undrunk beer.

"Does he make any money at it?" I asked. "Oh." Harry thought a moment. "He gets by. Probably as good as some who been laid off and have families."

He picked up a rag and wiped off the bar, unnecessarily. "He'll make a few bucks on what he's doing now—those cartoon things." Caricatures, he meant, but I didn't correct him. "Whatever they've set the guy up to pay."

Somebody had punched up "The Little Drummer Boy" on the juke box and we listened for a while. "His best stuff he doesn't really make anything off of," Harry volunteered, for him a loquacious remark.

Pause. He walked away a few steps and lifted a framed picture from the shelf beside the cash register, brought it back and handed it to me.

It was Harry, and it wasn't Harry. The face, round jowls, thinning hair were Harry but the rest was not—a trim important-looking man in gray business suit, vest and subtly striped tie. He was seated at an executive desk in a high-backed black-leather chair, mahogany paneled wall behind.

"Chairman of the Board," Harry laughed, embarrassed. The portrait was mixed media, water color with inked highlights, had the look of oil.

"Funny thing," Harry began, speaking out of some need to explain, "it's not how anybody would picture me, except Paul." He waited while I examined it more. "Had an effect on me. I've always thought about buying this place, you know, from the guy that owns it. But that's all. When Paul did this thing it got me to thinking maybe I could, you know."

"I keep it over by the register to remind me to put some aside and it mounts up, you know?" He suddenly needed to look after some drinkers down the bar, and flee from the discomfort of his long speech.

When he returned I handed him back the portrait. "You oughta see what he did with Lillian. Made her look like that British princess, thin, you know, not like she is, or was. And, well, beautiful." Strange word for Harry. "She doesn't come in anymore, except afternoons once in a while. She works at that place where women exercise and get tanned. Looks great. She calls him Renoir."

Harry was on a verbal roll. "Virginia, over at Hinkle's, he did her with two kids in the picture. She hasn't got any. But just wait." He shook his head. "Now Cecil, he got mad, because Paul made a jockey out of him. Cecil's short."

"Understand, he don't charge for a portrait like that. Oh, he'll take whatever he can get when somebody wants one done from a snapshot. Like those." He pointed across the room to three unframed pastels tacked on the wall above the wainscoting. I went over to look. All women, glamourous poses, frayed on the edges. "They're girl friends, or ex-girl friends," he said when I came back. "Can't take them home so they stay here."

A hefty woman and two men in UK jackets came in the door, hailed Harry with Merry Christmas greetings that he returned nodding and smiling. They took seats at a table nearby, ordered beer and chasers. It took Harry a bit to fill the order and set the drinks on the bar to be picked up. When he came back to me he spoke in a lower, almost confidental tone. "Nobody ever knows when Paul's gonna do a real portrait of him. He just brings it in, when it's done, and I prop it up on the shelf till the subject comes in. Then they don't always take it home right away. Sometimes it looks like a goddammed gallery in here." I couldn't picture Harry in an art gallery, but you never know.

In the back, Paul was leaning back in his chair drinking his beer while the others passed around his sketch. Harry saw me looking. "He never drinks when he works, even when there is plenty. He can't buy a drink in here. And he gets some meals over at Hinkle's and gas. He does all right."

Harry stepped back, fell silent. He seemed talked out, the subject finished. I became aware that I'd been here a while, needed to get going.

"Well, see you, Harry. Merry Christmas." He nodded.

As I walked out the door I wondered what kind of portrait the artist might do of me. It was dark out now, and I still had the laundry to do. It had started snowing.

# 19 Here and There

A friend in Kansas City has a dog, Pukita the Akita, and two cats, Southpaw and Fastball, who are techies. Fastball likes to turn the FAX machine on and off and on and off and on and on—for the amusement of all, especially Pukita, who barks in time with the whir of the machine. The three are especially delighted when my friend goes off to work, sets the security alarm but forgets to put the animals in the basement. They dash around gleefully setting off the motion sensors, bringing the wail of police sirens into the neighborhood to break up the mid-day boredom.

Which brings to mind George, the town dog of Vevay (locals call it Vevee), a village 15 miles upriver. Not George, my beagle, although they are such kindred spirits they could have been country cousins. This George is a big overfed hound, part blue-tick, part something else, part white, part reddish brown. All Vevay is his turf; he knows everybody and everybody knows him. He goes by the IGA and the convenience store every day to collect bits of baloney and such that fellow citizens bring out when they pass the time of day with him. He hangs out some at the Post Office, sometimes makes the rounds with the mailman who says "George is the only dog in town that hasn't bitten me." When tourists take walking tours, George goes along as greeter and guide. If he gets tired he stretches out wherever it is that he got tired, and if that's in the street, well, people just drive around rather than wake him up.

When it's hot outside, George steps on the pad that opens the doors of the drug store and goes inside where it's cool to nap. One night the village police answered the automatic alarm at the store and found only George, who had wandered through a sensor beam and set off the alarm. Somebody had closed the store for the night and forgot to wake him up.

Some cranks got to complaining about stray dogs roaming around so the Town Council, eager to shut them up, hired a dog-catcher. They put him on the payroll on a Monday and by Thursday, guess who he had snared! George's owner bailed him out and tied him up in the backyard.

Soon George's friends got to missing him and they did some complaining of their own. To the dogcatcher, who took the stan-dard cop-out, "I was just doing my job." To the Council members, repeatedly. Said one, "I've caught a lot of flak from a flood of people." Caught between factions, the Council did as expected—nothing.

Not George's friends. They made George the Grand Marshal of the upcoming annual Wine Festival parade. Had him ride up front in a convertible so all could see who was Top Dog!

When hunting season opened that fall, guess who the game warden snared right off—the dogcatcher! He got fined $1,000 and costs on 16 counts of illegally killing and selling deer, lost the rifle he had used to shoot deer from the road at night with a flashlight, lost the handgun he carried, lost his hunting license.

\*\*\*

James Thurber, the late, great cartoonist and writer for New Yorker magazine, put it well in his book, <u>Thurber's Dogs</u>, when he said: "I am not a dog lover. A dog lover is a dog in love with another dog."

\*\*\*

News item:

Eggleston Elementary School will hold an Earth Day parade tomorrow in downtown Madison.

The children will carry banners and signs and will pull wagon floats. A kazoo band will play.

The procession will start at the school at 9:15 a.m. It will proceed west on the Main Street sidewalk to the Broadway Fountain. There the students of Lydia Middleton Elementary School will be waiting to see the parade.

The parade will return to Eggleston on the Third Street sidewalk.

\*\*\*

Hoosier basketball fervor knows no limits. A bipartisan fan who lives on the riverfront has mowed off a large grassy field across the road from his house. In the center are three flagpoles, with flower beds at their bases. In the middle is the red, white and blue of Old Glory. To one side is the crimson and white flag of Indiana University and on the other side the blue and white of the University of Kentucky.

On the morning after a basketball game, if IU or UK loses,

he lowers the appropriate flag to half staff. Leaves it that way all day.

He doesn't do that when either school plays a football game. Probably too much work, because they lose so often.

A fellow on Main Street has enclosed the parking place beside his house with a wrought-iron fence and a sign marking it "Bobby Knight Court." At Christmas time, he put up lights on his porch in the shape of a Christmas tree and I saw him trying to shape it into the IU logo (the "I" superimposed on the "U"). He'd stand back, study it, and make adjustments. The next night the entire decoration was gone.

\*\*\*

A windy rainstorm blew down a huge limb from a big, old tree in my neighbor's yard across the street, completely blocking off our street and denting the roofs of a couple of cars. Almost within the hour a cleanup crew arrived with chain saws and set about cutting and clearing. Minutes after the buzzing began, men emerged from houses all up and down the block, armed with power saws and a purposeful look. The neighborhood hummed and in no time the obstacle was removed, the debris hauled away, and the sawyers were looking around for more wood to conquer.

\*\*\*

Sign above the registration desk in a small hotel:
> Dogs are welcome in this hotel. We never had a dog that smoked in bed and set fire to the blankets. We never had a dog who stole our towels, played the tv too loud and had a noisy fight with his traveling companion. We never had a dog that got drunk and broke up the furniture. So if your dog can vouch for you, you're welcome, too.

\*\*\*

The mail brings my electric bill with the usual insert brochures that inform about all the marvelous services and the wonderful work the company is providing. I am especially gratified by this month's insert entitled, "Trees and Reliable Electric

Service."

Up until now it was my fervent conviction that no force on earth could butcher a tree like the utility company, under the guise of trimming it. We have a certain amount of evidence in the neighborhood to substantiate my claim. The company often describes the extensive training given its employees to assure the utmost in friendly service to us consumers. I had been about to offer the friendly suggestion that utility company executives could use some training in landscape aesthetics.

Now I am relieved to learn of the noble purposes behind the "vegetation management program" being carried out by "professional line-clearing contractors". They follow a directional pruning method promoted by the National Arborist Association. All that cutting not only prevents interruption in our electrical service but it is good for the trees. Those hideous cuts that slash open trees from the top that you see along the highway are "V-cuts" that reduce unsightly growths. The L-cut that slices off the top half leaves fewer wounds on the tree. And so on.

How wrong I have been. I am sorry now that we didn't do something about those wasps in one of our trees that stopped the professional line clearers cold. But I still think the aesthetics course would be a good idea.

\*\*\*

My biggest thrill in a long time happened one afternoon when I was jogging at the water's edge on the Kentucky side of the river. I came upon a high boulder, half in the water. Looming just visible behind was the smooth white head, piercing eye, and hooked beak of a huge bird. A bald eagle! As I neared, it slowly rose with a powerful surge of long wings, soared silently, calmly downriver and alighted in a tree. There it watched as I passed beneath, slowed to a walk. The American eagle! A sight like that can make your days for months to come.

# The Fifth Book of George

The injustice of being a convicted miscreant is that good behavior goes unnoticed while the first slip from the path of purity brings retribution in full measure. I had gone straight for three years, six months and 21 days since taking a fall for allowing Amigo to stray. She and Sandy were sticking close to home, their wanderlust satisfied by long outings twice a day. We altered our routes drastically to avoid the most zealous property defenders, usually loaded up in the car to take off for woods or cemetery or golf course or riverbank. Only George's beagle instincts required more roam and it is true that twice I had to claim him at the animal shelter after he had been picked up for straying, ratted on by vigilantes. I got away with just paying for his keep and figured this was the Lord's way of returning him under our joint custody agreement.

Now I was done in, again for a technically true but hardly flagrant infraction. George had been hanging around at the Canidas' in the next block because Cupcake, their Lhasa apso, was in heat. She was being kept inside. The Canidas, lovely people, didn't mind George plighting his troth but their next-door neighbor had called the law. She's a fussy woman who believes that every yellowed blade of grass in her yard is the work of some unsanitary canine.

So George, snared in his amorous stupor, got carted off to

the slammer. This time when I went to retrieve him I was presented with a citation to answer for my crime.

As before, when I approached the bar Mr. Justice Hoying was surprised to see me. I proffered my summons, obviously the only paper before him for my case. This time I didn't make the mistake of incriminating myself by volunteering a description of the episode.

Forgetting I was practically a recidivist, I grumbled about the prospect of being convicted by a slip of paper, no prosecuting witness, no trial.

"You want a trial?" retorted the judge. "I'll give you a trial."

He was no doubt perturbed himself about defendants showing up without notice. I should have kept my mouth shut; truth does not always serve.

I fell into a silent mercy-of-the-court mode and he recovered his judicial/political demeanor. After some irrelevant pleasantries, he said he'd get back to me.

I walked out wondering if Judge Hoying was ready for a seat on the Supreme Court.

A year went by with no word and I moved back to the view that Judge Hoying was a legal giant who could differentiate between justice and technical guilt. Then, one morning in May, George took off at the crack of dawn for his neighborhood rounds and did not return.

I waited out the next several days; no George. I called the shelter; no George. The three-week in-heat time for female canines passed; no George.

I knew he'd show up; he always had before.

Amigo and Sandy didn't seem to notice his absence; George always had his own agenda. I tried to take confidence from them but forty times a day I glanced down at the square pane of glass at the bottom of the French doors where his face would be framed when he whined to come in. I knew that whine like a mother hears her baby's first cry over any other sound. I'd think I heard it, then realize I hadn't. The faint sound of lapping at the water dish outside the door sent me to see and be disappointed it was another dog drinking, not George.

He couldn't be dead, his body would have been found and reported by someone, unless he'd been hit by a speeding car on a highway, flung into a ditch and left for dead.

The notice in the mail summoning me to trial was a jolt but the judge had said, a year before, that he'd get back to me. I made the familiar trip to court, saw through the courtroom door that the judge hadn't arrived but sitting at the prosecution table were the animal control warden and a court clerk, waiting.

A gray-suited young man approached me in the hall, asked if I was the defendant in the case and identified himself as the city attorney. In a surreptitious voice he began the venerable plea-bargain pitch, useful to any ambitious prosecutor needing a high conviction rate to advance his political career. From a sheaf of paper he noted that I had "a prior conviction" and warned that "a second offense" could result in a fine of $3,000, a figure never mentioned when the judge had first educated me that "allowing an animal to stray" was only a quasicriminal offense.

I said the offense had occurred more than a year ago and the dog was now probably dead. The attorney stared implacably at the floor.

I was trapped, they were ready for me. When I nodded my acceptance of the prosecutor's deal of $1 fine and costs for a guilty plea, he agreeably arranged that I wouldn't have to wait for the judge. Costs had gone up since my prior conviction, $53 on top of the fine. Justice must be served; it is blind, occasionally it is tempered with mercy, but always the books must be cleared.

The waiting for George went on and each outing with Amigo and Sandy became a search mission. We revisited every place we had explored and where he had ranged far from my usual track into thickets and up ridges I plunged and climbed, called and whistled. In some places his image haunted me. Along a deep, dry creek bottom I remembered him trotting from a bushy concealment with a rabbit in his mouth. I'd heard no howl of recognition, no commotion, figured he'd found a dead rabbit because he'd never caught one before. He was so proud he half strutted over the stones and sand of the creek bed, head erect, carrying his trophy home. After some distance, the burden became tiresome so he sneaked off and buried the carcass behind a bush.

When it came time to load up in the car, Amigo and Sandy crawled into their customary places in back but George's side of the front seat was noticeably empty. With no long wait for him to finish his investigations I drove off feeling we were leaving early. Often we stopped at the Dairy Queen for refreshment following a prolonged trek. Now I recalled how he'd finish his cone and then get half of mine. We didn't stop there as much as before.

I searched for George in my imagination, visualizing places he might have gone we hadn't covered. Sometimes I dreamed about him finding me, as it usually happened.

Not knowing George's fate softened my despair and prolonged my hope. I empathized with those families whose loved ones are still missing in action in war who demand a final, certain report. They are clinging to hope. Not knowing is a strange and mixed blessing; uncertainty preserves the flicker of hope while the reality of loss eases its gradual acceptance.

As weeks ran into months my awareness of George's absence diminished. After a period of not thinking of him I'd feel guilty, as if thinking could bring him back. And always there were unexpected reminders. Folk along our route asked, "Where's the beagle?" and freshed the ache of his loss. A woman who missed seeing George was adamant against the notion that he could have been killed. She insisted he must have been stolen, a genuine possibility. Dog thieves make off with beagles for sale to hunters or pharmaceutical firms that use them as research animals. It was a prospect almost worth grasping; at least he might still be alive.

By the one-year anniversary of George's departure it seemed time to mark his passing, more to honor his memory than to acknowledge his death. Memorial Day approached, a suitable time for an observance. I decided to plant a tree in his memory. Mary provided a white ash sapling that I placed in the center of a small rose garden I was trying to grow in the backyard.

I bought a dog collar with a plate inscribed "In Memory of George" to be fastened around the young tree's trunk, loose with room for growth. I wrote a ceremony in four parts. On a warm, sunny Memorial Day we gathered to pay our respects and dedi- cate the George Memorial Tree.

As each part was read, granddaughter Sara, who missed George so terribly she dreamed about him and woke up crying, stepped tentatively forward and dropped a memory bone at the base of the seedling.

The words of the eulogy were unashamedly sentimental, spoken to him, expressing our memories and feelings for him.

"We remember you, George, your rugged stance and torn ear. . .when you came to us it was by your choice. . .we see you standing at the end of the driveway, deciding whether to come in. . .we can hear your howl. . .how you watched the river lap against the shore. . .Everybody asks about you.. .wonders where you've gone. . .all your friends miss you. . .when you left that day, we waited and waited, searched all over. . .every once in a while we find one of those bones that you hid. . .we know that your Heavenly Master will let you run free and forgive you when you are late coming home.. .you will not be any stray dog but have a special place by His side."

Ten quiet, sober minutes. When I looked up from our circle around the tree a group had gathered, 12 or 15 people, neighbors, strangers, who somehow heard of the ceremony and came. George had friends he didn't know about. He'd become a neighborhood legend.

There was lift from sadness in the brief recognition of a stray dog that was now a Hound of Heaven. Comfort, too, bringing uncertainty to a close. Still, I would not have been surprised one day to hear that whine and find him at the door. I would say, "Come on in, George. Where have you been?"

SQUEAKY

# 20 Squeaky

They are a feisty pair, small black Labs, identical brother and sister. When we draw within scent or sight they come charging from the long open yards of houses lining the county road, barking indignantly. At the road they hesitate, notice how much bigger Sandy and Amigo are, and stand off giving us what-for.

Amigo likes the little male, trots out to socialize. That brings him across the road into the field where we pass through but his sister waits behind.

Most times they emerge from one or another of the houses set back from the road but I can't place where they belong. We've encountered them upriver in the woods, always together, keeping their distance. Occasionally the male will join my dogs in their prowl but the female stays apart. If the two get too far separated, she sets up a frightened howl and the brother returns to her side.

Mystery dogs. People along that section of the river are aware of them but are certain only that they're strays and have been around a long time. Their origins vary by the telling.

First I was told they are wild dogs, abandoned by a pack as pups left in a cave on a ridge above Bennett's Landing. They survived on their own, sleeping under wreckage of rusty barges, hunting their food. Inseparable, like orphans in the storm. A colorful, apocryphal story.

Later I learned that Ric, a worker at Bennett's Marina, had been leaving food out for them. And householders along the road often tossed out scraps that were gone the next morning. Same way with me; I put a dog dish under a picnic shelter in a meadow, filled it when we made our run. The Labs would watch, never come near as I poured in the chow, but the dish was empty the next trip.

In winter, one fellow left the door of his pickup truck ajar for the dogs to climb in and sleep in some warmth on cold nights.

Eventually I pieced together the likely truth. The little black dogs were dropoffs, abandoned as puppies along the highway above Bennett's. Ric had found the box the disposers had left them in. When he tried to catch them, the pups scattered into the brush. So he began leaving out food.

One spring the river rose and the dogs were trapped on a small island of ground surrounded by high water. Ric rescued the male, despite some fierce resistance, so he shut him in the cab of his truck. Then he went back for the female. Once free of the water, she jumped from his arms and ran away. Ric went back to his truck, thought holding onto the male might draw his sister, but the snappy little dog put up such a fuss Ric let him go.

The sight of creatures running free offends some humans. If it's a stray, call and have it picked up. If it's wild, shoot it.

A woman who lives on the highway did both. She called for the county conservation officer to come out and get rid of the Labs. He tried to catch them but couldn't. So the woman got a gun and shot both dogs. Killed the female and wounded the male in the leg. He limped away screaming and disappeared.

He survived. Ric could hear him at night up on the ridge, howling mournfully for his sister.

I'd missed the Labs for several weeks, not knowing about the shooting. Then one day the male turned up alone, stayed with us as we explored, and followed us home.

He hung around a while, then left. Almost every day he repeated the pattern, joined us at the customary place, stayed closer than usual during the hunt and tagged along when we came home. He drank from the outside water dish like the others, shared in the bone parties we had after a long run. He was at ease with Amigo and Sandy but wary of me.

One morning when we came out he was there. Again the next morning, he emerged from the backyard where he'd discovered the dog house. He stayed on, fell into our routine, ran with us, heartily ate the food I put out for him, sneaked inside to eat from the dogs' dishes.

Occasionally when the others were napping he'd vanish for a time, then return. Amigo and Sandy accepted him naturally, accorded him the forbearance of equals, no more, no less. He had found a family. He was now our stray-in-residence, following in the tradition of Boomer, Bart and George.

An elderly couple approached me in the grocery store the other day and asked, "Did George ever come back?" They waited with such expectant hope I was reluctant to answer, "No, he never did." Their faces showed disappointment. "We miss him," said the woman. George's absence was still noticed, more than two years after he disappeared.

Was the little black Lab another George? Both had suffered at the hands of humans, both had survived as hunters and scroungers, both were streetwise, each had a resonant howl but the Lab's whine was more of a squeak, like a rubber duck. When neighbors noticed him around and asked his name, I replied offhandedly, "Squeaky." Although it violated all my rules for naming a dog, the name stuck.

Like George, Squeaky's merging with us was gradual, as if he stood outside the circle in safety, watching and waiting before stepping inside. He would move toward me, sniff my shoes, but if I reached or stepped toward him, he ran. He ventured inside the house, even dozed in a corner unless I closed the door, cutting off his escape. Then he paced and squeaked until I opened the door and let him out. Once assured his freedom, he came in again. Leaving the door open was a simple enough remedy in mild weather, something else when it was cold outside.

On our outings I picked up signs of his earlier life struggle. He hunts but has a poor nose, often misses game darting out ahead of him. He seeks birds mostly, river geese and pigeons, many already dead that he finds. Then instinctively he carries them to a secluded place and carefully buries them, storing provender for lean times ahead. Any sound resembling a gunshot sends him scrambling for cover, into the house if we are there.

The little black Lab who just wants to be left alone seems hexed. On one bad trip, he fell into a four-foot pit, couldn't get out until I reached to help and he scrambled to the top; was attacked by a Doberman pinscher that had slipped his leash and whose owner blamed Squeaky; was screeched at by a killdeer he hadn't even noticed. Kids chase him, wanting to "pet the doggie" and he flees. Once a pit bull had him by the leg and I was about to kick its ribs in before the owner pulled him off.

The animal hater across the street showed up at my door and handed me a heavy black plastic bag that he claimed was a deer carcass that Squeaky had buried in his yard. The package weighed four times what Squeaky did; he always buries his game on the riverbank, and besides, how could little Squeaky bring down a deer? All this logic came to me only after the irate neighbor had walked off, leaving me holding the bag.

No wonder Squeaky's countenance is a sad, suspicious look, ever on guard.

He's an outside dog, given to two or three-day furloughs from our midst. He's easy to leave. When a piece of work took me away every day for several months Mary came over at midday to let Amigo and Sandy out for a breather but there was no worry about Squeaky; he'd fend for himself.

I rely on the looseness of his connection with me as an out if the vigilantes get active. He's not my dog, I will say; he's just a stray who hangs around.

As his residency lengthens, Squeaky is imperceptibly learning from grooving. He waits at street crossings for my signal to cross because the other dogs do. He never pees in the house because the others don't. Once inside when his stomach was upset he came to me and whined, clearly uncomfortable. I opened the door and once outside he threw up.

Word has come to me that two neighbor ladies are leaving food out for him. He's taken to coming upstairs to sleep behind my desk while I'm working. He likes country music on the radio, gets up and leaves if I switch to a classical station. Sometimes he startles me by sending up a forlorn howl, maybe a lament for his lost sister. I've awakened from a nap on the couch to discover he has carried my shoes or slippers out into the yard, a sign of bonding.

Every day it becomes more undeniable—I've been adopted again.

# 21 Grooving

It is spring enough now for Homo sapiens to emerge from their households, sniff the mild air, squint the sunshine and wander about their habitat assessing the wear of winter. Hard, exhausting weather has left a residue of bleached grass, matted brown leaves, dead remnants of last season's plants and sticks littered beneath the bare trees. A few grass tufts show early green and the yellow blossoms of crocuses and daffodils remind the lodge-dweller that it is time to set about improving on nature.

The first migrating RVers are arriving at the city campground to hook up, put out their awnings and satellite dishes and prepare their summer nestings by the water. Along the two-mile riverside stretch of Vaughn Drive a new flow of slow-moving vehicles passes suggestively, radios throbbing, as the town's youth initiate the vernal mating ritual. This traffic is complicated by their elders who, tired of just sitting in the house, get out and drive around just sitting in the car.

The dogs and I meet this annual emergence with ambivalence. We welcome the spirit lift of spring, but on our travels now we must deal with congestion and cantankerous humans from whom we have been blessedly free in the cold months of their hibernation.

There are exceptions. A cheerful woman out examining the state of her rose bushes smiles and says, "Pretty day, isn't it?" and goes on to say that she sees us pass by almost every day, crossing through the little covered bridge over the creek in the valley below her house. She always counts the dogs until all are accounted for. She has noticed how well they mind me, waiting at the street in front of her house until I give the word that it is all right to cross.

What a perceptive lady.

Another afternoon I stop in the alley across the street to chat with the retired schoolteacher as she pulls dead honeysuckle vines from her japonica bush. The dogs hover around, sit or lie down, Sandy and Amigo close by wondering why humans talk so much. She remarks on how well behaved the dogs are, waiting for me without fuss. She marvels at the way they stay with me when we pass by on the walk, maybe one trotting ahead and another dragging behind but all moving at my pace. She could never get her dog to do that.

For someone retired, she has certainly kept her figure.

Coming up the sidewalk on Walnut Street one morning we approach a shiny police car parked mysteriously at the curb. The young officer inside smiles and says hello. Apprehension rises in me; is this official courtesy or has he spotted me as a two-time loser? He notes that my dogs are not on a leash, but wonders how I control them so well. He is new to the force, says that when he was breaking in riding double his partner saw us on the riverfront, pointed us out and said, watch, see how his dogs stop at the street and wait until he signals before they cross. "That guy has more control over his dogs than a lot of people who walk theirs on a leash," the officer said.

Without question, two of Madison's finest.

Dogs that mind, well behaved, under control. It could be that their exemplary behavior is obvious to right-thinking observers and these accolades for my guidance are deserved. It could be, also, that a blind squirrel will stumble across an acorn once in a while.

The question that punctured my pride is how these orderly manners came about. Not by my training; I had so failed in my aborted attempt at obedience training of Amigo that I made no effort with the others.

How then? By osmosis? Well, yes, in a way. As I scanned the years with my dogs for some model of rearing it came clear that my methods were more evolution than instruction. On-the job training, made up as I went along to suit the need and circumstances that arose. As much serendipity as intention, but worthy of study.

I knew from adult education that no new model of learning can gain credibility without a polysyllabic title and a euphonic acronym. But I couldn't think of any. So I shall call my approach *Grooving*.

By imparting this marvel of effective dog training for posterity I am compelled to enter a caveat: Grooving works for me but may not work for anybody else. It is no one-size-fits-all standard brand of step-by-step instruction. Execution is simple but requires time and perception.

Grooving evolves from empirical principles not universally accepted by the canine establishment. The primary principle is that learning is mutual for both dog and human. The other principles:

<u>Not all dogs are alike.</u> Dogs differ by age, breed, sex, temperament, size and past experience. A puppy is a blank slate ready for the marks of training. But the pooch who has been around a few years has done some learning of her own, and may take some unlearning. The mutt rescued from the shelter, while every bit as intelligent as his pedigreed cohort, may have life episodes that mar his learning readiness.

In adult education a theory called *andragogy* sets apart the training of adults from *pedagogy*, the teaching of children.

Andragogy holds that adults bring a load of life into training, including emotional baggage, that must be reckoned with but that can be a base upon which to build further learning. Despite the theory some teachers, particularly college professors, continue to treat adult learners like children, just as some animal trainers treat all dogs as puppies.

Amigo was two years old (a teenager in dog time) when we joined up and she had experienced abuse, confinement and separation from her master. Sandy had suffered the trauma of a drop-off puppy and came to me as an adolescent refugee from divorcing owners. George's past as a stray was known only to him but he learned enough survival skills to get by until he decided to spend his prime adult years with us. What training program fits these three? It is said that you can't teach an old dog new tricks. If not, old dogs face a dubious future. Retraining is possible, but an individualized unorthodox approach is necessary.

<u>Not all dog owners are alike.</u> If the interaction between human and animal is the core of dog training then the inevitable differences among the keepers of 54 million dogs in this country must render a same-for-all procedure unlikely to succeed. Yet in my study of dog training I found almost no acknowledgement that humans who have dogs might differ. The same lofty prescription for firmness, kindness, consistency, patience, control, discipline and so on was written for all.

Even if a conscientious dog person aspired to all those noble attributes, circumstance could forestall their achievement. She works for a living and can't find time for daily obedience lessons or brushings or long walks. He is a softy who can't bring himself to correct the little pest that barks so much. What of the macho man who growls and snaps even more than Rover?

Time is a trainer. Not one evening a week for a couple months or a weeklong send-away crash course that gets training done quickly. Rather the ongoing, long-haul living together of owner and animal is the course of learning for the two. Grooving is possible because of the time I spend with my dogs. I am with them more than I am not, too much in fact. If work or chores take me away, after a few hours I feel the need to get back, like a working mother worrying about her kids at home.

Before Sandy and George joined us, a death in my family took me away from Amigo for a week. She was well cared for by Mary, slept on a shirt of mine in Mary's spare room, spent days in her own yard—most of the time sitting by the fence gate, waiting. After a few days she wouldn't eat. When I returned it would be difficult to say who was most relieved, Amigo, Mary or me.

The time I spend with my canine crew is inordinate, but not rare, when one considers the number of single citizens with a dog or the folk who insist upon taking the four-legged member of the family with them wherever they go. Such constancy forges a connection so strong it becomes a channel that carries the intentions of human to animal, like osmosis. For good or ill, dog and owner are grooving together.

Let dogs be dogs. We humans, some of us at least, have an almost irresistible urge to play God, to make dogs over in our own image. We breed them to our purposes and whims, crop their coats to keep them cute and forever young, dress them in designer outfits with jewelry and dark glasses. We teach them stupid pet tricks like singing, playing piano or basketball. We expect them to behave like tea-party guests, are horrified if a dog gets dirty or snoops into garbage. Such anthropomorphism run amuck is epitomized by the "continental cut" that gives French poodles fur bracelets and pompoms resembling a Parisian prostitute.

Grooving begins by regarding a dog as a dog, not as a four-legged human. By accepting certain behavior as natural, the temptation to expect humanlike comportment is reduced and the training load eases accordingly. One needs to admit that dogs are social animals drawn to other dogs and sniffing is their greeting; they bark, sometimes at strangenesses not recognized by humans; they like to roam around, chase cats, dig in dirt, drink out of puddles, hunt critters, eat smelly stuff, pee where they're not supposed to, scratch when they itch. It's all in their job description.

A movement fostered by pet periodicals would turn every dog into a Canine Good Citizen by requiring him to pass a 10-part test to assure behavior acceptable to landlords, insurance companies, legislators and the media. An outstanding concept! Too valuable to be to limited to dogs, a Human Good Citizen classification should be instituted forthwith. Evaluation questions could include: Does the subject vote? Does he pay taxes without howling? Does she answer when called for jury duty? Does the subject refrain from attacking other breeds because they are different? Does she chase after cars that are exceeding the speed limit? Does he avoid dumping on the environment?

By nature, dogs are pack animals and here grooving offers a bonus: Dogs will train other dogs. Under pack hierarchy, the alpha dog leads the others. Dogs regard their human family as a pack and their owner as alpha dog. I was alpha to Amigo. When George and Sandy joined the pack they naturally looked to Amigo as beta dog. I was pack commander, she was second in command and the others were the enlisted personnel.

This chain of command requires no insignia of rank or table of organization. When we go on maneuvers Amigo takes her orders from me, usually ahead on the point. I direct where to go, when to stop, where to reverse course and so on. Amigo follows my orders and the other dogs follow her lead.

Moreover, when other dogs join up, they instinctively submit to our command structure. I've taken to the field with a pack of five or six dogs and found them surprisingly manageable.

Even more remarkable is the spontaneous learning. Temporaries attached for even occasional marches soon fall into our line of advance, stopping at streets, avoiding off-limits areas or soaking in the river at the customary-places. Strays with no apparent housebreaking who follow inside never offend the floors; it just isn't done by the pack.

Certainly we have occasional freelance activity. George, who always ranged farther afield and frequently chose to patrol on the other side of the street, did not tempt the rest; they knew he was under special orders. However, the appearance of a rabbit or possum put a strain on our discipline.

The fewer rules the better. Business has a quaint concept known as "management by exception" which means approximately, "If it ain't broke, don't fix it." Such a hands-off philosophy is out of sync in our automated society where each task is analyzed, segmented, timed, and programmed, then micromanaged by software. Training is equally trivialized by breaking performance down into pieces that can be identified, taught, practiced, evaluated and then reassembled for use when needed.

Some dog owners are prone to mindless overcorrection. I cringe when a dog barks for good reason and is shouted at or slapped. Or a sociable pooch strolling with his mistress shows curiosity about a nearby dog, slows to take a look and gets a sudden sharp yank on his leash and orders to behave (that is, to stop being a dog). The most dysfunctional owner's correction is calling a dog to come and if he doesn't comply immediately, bawling him out when he does. Constant correction can have a boy-who-cried-wolf effect; pointless commands teach the animal to disregard all commands as hopeless.

Grooving all but eliminates commands, simplifies management and makes the human-dog relationship much more pleasant. I've found minimal need for words of control. Stop or Wait was perhaps my only mandatory command.

Others I use from time to time are Hush, Drop It, Let's Go and This Way. When a strange cur wanders up and mine go tense, I may order Put Your Back Down.

The words really don't matter; their meaning does. My dogs have come to know what I mean no matter what I say, from my tone, the situation, their own learning. Even my most essential command, Wait, for when we are crossing a street, may come out as Hold On or Not Yet and still be observed. That's the only command I repeat, to hold them until I release them with O.K. or Here We Go. It is the sound in my voice and my example that they obey.

I've gone days without uttering a single instruction. They've learned where to go and where not, when to stop. They may look to me for direction, as at a fork in the road, to ask Which Way? Then a hand signal will do.

Fewer commands assures more control when needed. If a potentially dangerous situation arises they know from the louder, more demanding tone of my voice to take heed. Mild-mannered Sandy is a snake hunter. She is adroit and quick and keeps shaking the snake so furiously that the chance of a bite is slight. But twice she has grabbed up a venomous copperhead and when I roared "Drop It!" she immediately flung it away.

Grooving eschews mastery for the sake of mastery and saves control for emergencies.

An unrestrained dog is a calm dog. You recall that Russian fellow named Ivan Petrovich Pavlov who decided one day to fool his dog. He offered the mutt a juicy morsel and at the same time rang a bell, right when the dog was slobbering in anticipation. After repeating the routine several times Pavlov could just ring the bell and the dog would drool. It was a dirty trick teasing the brut that way but Pavlov had bigger things in mind. He wrote up his pet trick in a scientific journal and gave it the name of "conditioned response." It proved, Pavlov said and everybody believed him, that you can induce a response even if there isn't any bone.

Dog people get their bells rung regularly by the animal-control cabal, and respond with Pavlovian persistency. In a conditioned rush to comply, dogs get caged, tied up, fenced in, chained, leashed, kept inside, hunted down, incarcerated and destroyed. Restraint so dominates the human-dog connection and defines the standard of training that the needs of the dog get forgotten.

Dogs need exercise, especially bigger ones. Most city dogs get precious little. If some owners weren't regulated by Rex's need to "go out," he might never get out of the house. Here is faithful Fido home alone all day who greets his human family as if they have been gone all year and finally gets taken for a walk, on a leash, for a couple of blocks. Big deal.

Both biology and exercise may be served by a fenced yard but if Spot has the agility he was born with he may defeat a fence, so then he is tied up as well as fenced in. Every day we visit canine neighbors whose whole world is the radius of a short chain. They are lonely, bored, angry, often without water, lucky if someone feeds them. The dictates of "responsible pet ownership" keeps the animal in solitary confinement.

Another dictum of behavioral science is the frustration-aggression concept. Much undesirable canine behavior—excessive barking, running wild when loose, refusing to obey, growling, biting—could be frustration turned to aggression. If so, more restraint will not solve much. The converse may be more true, that freedom from restraint, and a touch of tender loving care, calms a dog and makes it more controllable.

Perfect love is a verb, not a noun. The love of a dog for a human is unlimited and unconditional. It is offered whether we are rich or poor, smart or not, homely or handsome, of whatever color, size, shape, age or status, whether we are deserving or not. It comes as close to perfect love as we are apt to get.

Grooving requires expressions of human-to-animal love beyond food and keep that are simple and easy—touch, talk and play.

The Hungarian hussars would rub their horses ears and tail to revive the steed's flagging spirits after a demanding charge. Plains Indians touched a horse on every square inch of its body until it was soothed. The touching is light, not massage, a circular movement of the fingertips starting at the ears, nostrils, and tail. Some Indians could "break" a wild horse for riding by gentle, calming touch, not as theatrical as the cowboy outlasting the bucking bronco, but just as effective.

Dogs respond to touch with a pleasure approaching delirium. Samantha is a border collie who jumps up on the fence of her yard when we pass for a greeting, some ear and neck scratching and an oatmeal cookie. She makes clear that she prefers the scratching by refusing the cookie until she has received her ration of touching.

A mere hand on a dog's head will curtail excited barking sooner than the gruffest "Shut up!" Sandy wakes me too early some mornings, not to go out, but for some scratching on the neck underneath her chin. This can be administered with an almost indiscernible motion of fingers, while half asleep, sufficient to satisfy and send her, and me, back for more sleep.

Dogs like to hear some talk besides commands and reprimands and they are attentive listeners. Tag, the police dog of my youth, made regular Saturday morning visits to the Rev. Mr. Porte, pastor of the Brethern Church a block from our house. His taking off Saturdays on his own before I woke up was a mystery until Reverend Porte owned up. He took Tag into his study and practiced his Sunday sermon on him. Tag sat and listened intently, he said, ears drooping back at the hellfire parts but alert all the way through, more than he could say for some of his human flock. Tag was the most sanctified dog in town.

Some people discuss weighty problems with their dogs, counting on an appreciative hearing. Dog talk is most unifying when it matches their moods. "Gee that feels good," when one rolls in the grass scratching his back or "I'm coming" when they've run ahead and turn to 'see what's keeping me. Small talk about the snow, the cat that won't come down from that tree, or the need to close the door when it's cold outside is not lost on dogs. They understand when the subject is relevant. But try explaining that we can't go out because it is raining, or after 23 walks try talking sense to that whelp sitting bright-eyed waiting for No. 24.

Every dog is entitled to its own versicle. A song, a rhyme, brief and nonsensical, even a bit of doggerel. "Georgie Porgie pumpkin pie/Kissed the girls and made them cry" sent him into a wiggle of appreciation. "Sandy Andy Pandy" is enough to make her turn and listen. Repeated often, such silliness sets a tone of fun that dogs enjoy. Very good for humans, too, especially sobersides.

Humans also need play and dogs are happy to help. Getting down on the floor for a romp causes some canine uncertainty at first but once used to it, they don't want to quit. Chasing is fun, when they find out you can't catch them, and there's fetch and catching a frisbee or ball or stealing your socks or slippers.

For fear of offending some rule of decorum, many dog people shy from terms of endearment. Too bad; dogs love them. When Amigo pays her morning call on Georgia, she gets called "darlin'" or "sweetheart" and returns for more. Periodically Amigo goes across to visit Mary and you can hear her greeting, "Amigo, darling!" all over the neighborhood. At home, whenever Amigo hears Mary's voice from afar, her tail thumps.

For grooving to succeed, a dog needs benevolent attention from others besides her owner. Amigo's transformation from a fearful, shy abuse victim to an outgoing, friendly, people-curious creature could not have happened without the active caring of Mary, Georgia and others.

As I was poised to offer Grooving to the world I came across a pamphlet at the vet's announcing a "natural behavior management system" entitled PROMISE, said to be "scientifically designed" by a veterinary professor and an obedience instructor based on a dog's instincts. Available through your veterinarian at an unstated price.

These things happen, great minds toiling separately arriving at identical truth. And I hadn't even starting shooting my video yet.

# 22 Saying Goodbye

Time for our autumn poetry reading at the laundromat. Willie brings his book and favors us with James Whitcomb Riley's "When the frost is on the punkin and the fodder's in the shock." We are unlikely art patrons but appreciate the apt images of our Hoosier poet which prepare us for the coming cold. Foliage has gone through its green, red, yellow, brown scene changes. The low sun bends shadows across the leaves on the ground and the chilly air requires a jacket. Idle leisure has given way to back-to-school, back-to-work rhythms. Few pleasure boats churn the river and only diehard golfers take to the brown fairways. The campground is empty of RVs; the summer sojourners back in more weatherworthy homes. Darkness falls early and lights come on sooner.

The dogs and I favor fall and the winter it brings because humanity moves inside and leaves the outside to us. Lawn tenders give up their grass to leaves and snow. Fewer people are out in the cold and those we encounter are a hardy, friendlier sort. The flow of motor traffic thins to trips of necessity. We endure harsher elements as small inconvenience in return for such freedom.

Our freedom has been limited by Squeaky's refusal to ride in the car. As an outside dog with inside privileges he draws the line on certain practices that experience has taught him to avoid, such as venturing close to moving, four-wheeled monsters. This eliminates some of our most intriguing explorations a distance away or across the bridge. Occasionally I load up Amigo and Sandy and head for far outings, feeling they should not be denied. But the betrayed hangdog look Squeaky puts on as we drive away makes it a guilt trip for me.

Dealing with dogs is much like raising kids; the most exacting test for any parent is the next-to-impossible goal of treating all equally. One way out of the dilemma is to withdraw privileges from all, which evens things out unfairly like company punishment. If I try this, it catches up with me.

Driving by myself past the Sunrise Golf Course half blanketed by snow and nary a golfer in sight, I envision Amigo and Sandy whining excitedly whenever we turned into the parking lot and their bolt from the car as soon as I opened the door. Sandy would tear down the hill for the creek and thicket below No. 10 green, where rabbits lurked. Amigo would take her time, sampling the snow, toss it up and prance in the cool white stuff. Here's where George had roamed afar, traceable only by his howl. Now I regret leaving the dogs behind and think to fetch Sandy and Amigo for a run around the course, whether Squeaky likes it or not. Caution stops me; Amigo is showing her age and might not enjoy the course as she once did.

She's almost nine years old, an old lady in dog time. Her muzzle long ago turned white and she seems frail, even for her slender frame. Arthritis has stiffened and slowed her down.

She's as eager as ever when we set out for a run but hangs close to me and shows little zest for exploring on her own. If a critter pops up in front she can still summon energy for the chase, but she gives up quickly. Back home she is tired and naps for hours. I've been shortening our trips.

Amigo's infirmities have caused me to ponder her past. The sleek black creature whose graceful presence was marred by her terror at the sudden sound of a ball bouncing or a car backfiring, whose timidity toward strangers held her back, has became a social animal. Her first moves were to her friends, calling on Mary and Georgia or trotting out to welcome the shy girl from the next block who rode her bike over for a visit. Ultimately, she sought out strangers, kids, other dogs—leaving my side to greet them. She'd always drawn the comment, "pretty dog." Now I was hearing, "friendly dog." Gradually she has overcome the abuse of her earliest years.

With me, she holds to a proud independence. She knows she is top dog and plays the part, expects deference from the others, and from me. She's the reliable elder who needs no special attention. Sometimes I neglect her because I can count on her. Our communication is minimal; she reads me, anticipates me, at times confidently challenges me.

In her dotage she became incontinent, an embarrassing condition for a fastidious dog like Amigo. Cortisone shots corrected the symptom but brought on estrus, odd because she was spayed years ago. This excited Squeaky but she would have none of him.

I began to reckon with her terminal state. I'd always believed in putting a dog down to relieve its suffering. A man down the block had a handsome silver shepherd so afflicted she had to drag her hind quarters around the backyard. His wife said he just couldn't bear to have the dog put to sleep. I vowed I would not be that way; I'd give a dignified animal a dignified death. I asked Mary if, when the time came, I could bury Amigo in the cemetery by the creek where Mary's dogs are buried, and where we had picnicked, and she agreed.

Now I faced the torment of knowing when her time had come. One wants, needs to take every measure to relieve suffering and prolong life. How much suffering is too much? And how much is her life prolonged only for me?

Some days on our morning run Amigo tired soon after we started, slowed and then stopped, exhausted. I let her rest, then walked her home. She didn't mind when I resumed the run without her. One morning, she reached only the bottom of the hill leading into the park, gave out there and I carried her home. After that, she made no effort to come along.

I took her to the veterinarian, who advised keeping her for a few days so he could watch and treat her. When I went to visit her, she was listless, barely acknowledged me. I walked with her, slowly, in the yard outside. On the fourth day, he said she seemed to be improving, had put on some weight. But when I brought her in from our walk, she collapsed just inside the door and had to be carried to her cage.

The next day when I came in from the morning run with Sandy and Squeaky there was a message on the answering service to call the vet. When I reached him, he said, "Amigo died last night."

This couldn't be! I was to bring her home on Monday. I was hoping to have her around for spring, maybe summer—just laying around in the yard.

He said she may have had a heart attack. No! I <u>had</u> to have her back. Only for a few minutes. There was so much I had to say to her, do for her.

For a long time I walked around aimlessly, blanked. Sat down, got up, walked. The room is no different. The trees, the yard outside are the same. Sandy is sleeping; she doesn't <u>know</u>. Only a few words on the phone.

Then I broke, bawled, hard and awkwardly, tears closing my vision. The sobs reminded me of what I was crying about and brought more tears.

Mary offered the kindness of one who had known my loss. She said the ground at the farm was half frozen and we would need Gary to dig the grave. He was working a double shift at the power plant and wouldn't get off until Sunday at 4. I arranged to pick up Amigo's body Sunday morning.

She was wrapped in a black plastic bag, frozen hard. Her weight was not heavy to carry but her lifelessness was. I put her on the front seat of the car and drove home.

When I got there, I took her out of the bag and wrapped her in a colorful afghan she used to lie on when she was spry enough to climb up on the couch. Seeing her stiff, curled with head up, eyes closed as if asleep, jarred me finally to the reality that she was dead, gone.

Nothing to do now but wait for time to go to the farm. It was cold outside and I felt guilty about leaving her out there in the car while I was warm inside. I went out and sat with her, stroked her, tried to talk but all I could get out was, "Amigo, old girl." I said it again and again.

I couldn't leave her alone, so we went for a ride. I drove to where we had gone so often—along the railroad tracks by the river to the grain terminal, the deserted refinery and the country club golf course, up to the Hillside Inn where we had climbed the ridge, across the bridge to the high wood by the treatment plant and the creek where she drank and soaked. I talked to her about each place—the time she got lost on the ridge and found her own way home, the pigeons she flushed on the riverbank, the thick brambles she slipped through and waited for me, where dogs barked when we passed or came out to see us, the lot where we parked and met to go home, how I held her ice-cream cone as she licked it. I rested my hand on her head as I drove. Our last ride together, to all the familiar places.

Cold rain, almost sleet, began to fall as we drove to the farm. A slow, quiet trip. Sandy was silent in the back seat and the stillness of covered hump beside me was too evident.

After Gary broke through the hard crust of the ground in the grove by Big Creek, the shoveling was easier, mostly sand. I picked up a shovel and began digging and after a while, Gary said, very gently, "I'll get this. You go help Mary find some rocks." We went to the creek bank; most of the rocks were frozen in the ground.

I went back to help Gary. I wanted to help dig Amigo's grave. Four dogs were buried there, all German shepherds. Amigo would be next to Frisky, the matron who had ruled the rest with a sure direction.

When the hole was a good three feet deep and tamped down, I lined the bottom with a braid rug. Then I carried Amigo's body from the car and placed her on the rug.

I picked up a shovel and threw the first dirt on the body. As I did, Mary said simply, "She was a sweet dog."

We worked silently, filling the grave, placed rocks over it, turned one up for a head stone. Rain splashed on the rocks.

When we seemed to be finished, I said I wanted to read over her. We stood there, the three of us, wet, dismal, as I tried to read. I had written my last words to Amigo the night before.

"Well, Amigo, old girl, it is time to say goodbye." The word "goodbye" choked me; it was so final. I could hardly say, "And I don't want to."

Rain streaked the ink on the wilting paper in my hand. My lips quivered and garbled my words. Some lines I didn't finish. I sniveled like a baby, my voice whined and I was ashamed in the presence of this creature of poise and dignity.

Mary and Gary stood silent and patient. I had to force the final words through my sobbing.

"Goodbye.. .Amigo."

❋ ❋ ❋ ❋

We are still salt and pepper, but not a matched set. Sandy, the dazzler, attracting glances of admiration as white German shepherds can. Squeaky, the small black Lab half Sandy's size, who often goes unnoticed.

They are apart in temperament, too, yet blend as opposites often do. Sandy is a home dog, Squeaky a wanderer. She seeks the attention that he shuns. He is a hunter with a poor nose and difficulty capturing his prey. She gives chase only when the quarry shows itself but she has the killer instinct.

They are compatible because they don't compete, live together and with me in a kind of unremarkable harmony. They both sleep upstairs in my study. Squeaky goes up first, tired from a hard day, and curls underneath my desk or in a foot-square corner closed in by a bookcase and a chimney recess. Sandy must be wherever I am, crawls up on the couch to sleep while I'm there, only goes upstairs after I am in bed. She sleeps on a leather love seat almost made for her. Both are hard sleepers; they sometimes have to be roused in the morning.

We have worked out a smooth arrangement for our outings. We go together for the first run, to our customary retreats—up and down the riverfront, occasionally a foray into the streets and alleys. Squeaky roams and Sandy hovers near my course, unless some excitement draws her away, or when she takes her swim in the river.

He is a runner; she is a rider. When I have chores that require driving, I take Sandy along. She may just be lazy, she's content sitting in the back seat, head out the window taking in the passing scene. She appears to enjoy waiting in the parking lot while I shop, often is greeted by people passing who are amused to see a handsome dog peering from a car window. After this period of exclusive attention, she is willing to stay in the house and nap when I take Squeaky, still full of run, for a night walk.

The arrangement also keeps us out of trouble. It has been years since I have been snitched on and snared by the long arm of the law. I can't remember the last time I saw the dogcatcher. Perhaps it is because my amorous beagle is gone; perhaps my years here have completed my outsider's quarantine.

Ever since Amigo's death I've been trying to draw closer to Sandy. Not to replace Amigo, but to placate a tinge of guilt I've always had about neglecting Sandy. She was not a dog I chose, or one who chose me. I took her as a favor in what was to be a temporary stay that stretched into years. She was a full member of our triumvirate but she didn't have the seniority of Amigo, or George's spark and self reliance.

She was not easy to warm to. Sandy has little sense of humor, doesn't respond to invitations to romp and gives me a sobersided look when I call her "Wigglebutt" or recite her "Sandy Andy made out of candy" rhyme. She only tolerates affection, allows me to stroke and scratch her when she lies beside me on the couch, but seems relieved when I quit. Yet she wants to be close, to go along, be included, maybe from the insecurity of having three different owners in her lifetime.

Her clinging has irritated me at times and I suppose I show it because she gets a hurt dog look and tries fearfully to make amends when I blow my stack (which I have done on occasion, but have never struck a dog). The others would take it for the bluster that it was, withdraw from me until I cooled off, and then resume normal living. Dogs have infinite patience and abiding forgiveness.

I appreciated Sandy most when she ignored her meekness and showed some spirit: swimming for long stretches in the river as I walked along on the bank, getting after snakes, and barking at hot-air balloons and the moon.

In time I came to value her insistent closeness. When we made trips to my daughter's house and a reunion with the grand-daughter who had spent her toddler years with Sandy, she was a proper guest, quietly accepting attention, even tolerating Mac the cat. She dozed mostly, waiting for the time to leave. The highlight of the visit for her was climbing into the car and heading home. On the drive down the highway in the dark I talked to her, or we traveled in silence for miles, satisfied to be together.

Sandy never was a demanding dog. If she needed to go out, she sat silently at the door until I saw her there and let her out. She never begged for food but when it was dished out she ate ravenously. If I had to be away for several hours, standard procedure was to leave Squeaky outside and Sandy in the house. When I returned, she welcomed me happily, then went back to nap. A homebody.

Others noticed her decline before I did. I was with her too constantly to see the weight loss and her appetite was deceivingly healthy. When she began to tire on walks, and never left the yard when she could have, I realized that her nine years of life were telling on her. It was the arthritis of her breed and size that showed most; she couldn't climb up on the couch or into the car without help. She labored to slowly climb the steps to her upstairs bed, finally began sleeping downstairs, in a corner of my bedroom. When she lowered herself down she sometimes whimpered at the pain in her stiff limbs.

My father, a house painter, had arthritis in his later years and his doctor told him that climbing up and down ladders kept him from being crippled to immobility. The veterinarian said as much about Sandy, to keep her moving. I drove her to places where we could park close to the river and she went in for some surprisingly long swims. The vet said this was good physical therapy, that the energy required to dog paddle was much less than walking and the buoyancy of the water reduced strain on the legs. Sandy came out proud of herself, and slept soundly afterward.

I began to prepare myself for the time when I would have her put down. The hard question: when? How much discomfort is too much? I remembered that when people tried to console me on the loss of Amigo, they spoke of the good life I had given her.

That did not comfort me. What did was recognizing that her death was a merciful release from suffering. I would not let Sandy suffer if she didn't have to.

She made it easy for me. One day she did not leave the house at all, not even to urinate. The next morning I carried her out into the yard but she couldn't even squat down, she was so crippled and in pain. Her ribs protruded into my hand as I carried her back inside. I knew the time had come.

I phoned for an appointment with the vet, that day; I was afraid I might lose my nerve if I waited longer. I couldn't get in until five o'clock.

How we spend the hours awaiting the appointed time I can't recall, except that the final words and gestures I offered her brought no response; she was numbed by her distress.

We left with plenty of time for our final ride together—just as Amigo and I had visited the familiar places one last time, except that Sandy was alive. She was not in her usual place in the back; the ache she felt being lifted into the front was pain enough. We rode and I talked to her, when I could.

She slumped against the door, weary and without spirit for what passed outside the window. At times, she listened to me with her eyes. Her interest roused only when I managed some animation, as when we drew up at the end of the road to the woods by the long creek where she and Amigo and George had ranged so joyfully and I recounted, with forced laughter, her encounter with the skunk. Remembering those adventures of the happy hunters disheartened me; soon the last of them would be gone.

We parked by the grocery store over which had hovered the brightly colored hot-air balloon that she had barked at so determinedly, revealing for the first time her aversion to large objects overhead. We passed Sunrise Golf Course and I reminded her of the fun she's had there, but she stared blankly ahead. I stopped talking.

At Dr. Rimstidt's, I left Sandy in the car and went in to see if they were ready. He was in surgery and would be a few minutes. The woman behind the counter and the veterinary assistant spoke sympathetically to me.

We waited in the car. Sandy was quiet, holding still against the ache of movement. I searched for words of comfort or farewell and found none. I grew impatient, wished to get it over, and then felt guilty for wishing it.

Dr. Rimstidt emerged from a side door and came to the car. He offered to examine Sandy and questioned me about her condition, probing the need for euthanasia and the certainty of my decision. I was touched by his concern.

I carried Sandy inside and placed her, as tenderly as possible, on the examining table. A few words of instruction. An assistant held Sandy from behind and I put my arms around her head. Dr. Rimstidt held the syringe in his hand and then paused for a moment.

I looked into her eyes. My words came hard. "Goodbye, Sandy," I said. And then, "I love you."

She looked into my eyes, with love, with forgiveness. I knew she loved me but in that moment I finally felt that she knew I loved her. It was a precious moment. And then her sight faded out, and left peace.

# 23 Vision

*Where there is no vision, the people perish. Proverbs 29:18.*

During World War II, I spent some time—as we used to say—as "a guest of the German government." I was a *kriegsgefangener* at Stalag Luft 1 on the Baltic Sea, an edifying experience. To stave off boredom, limited rations, a trace of danger and the long uncertain wait for the war to end, many "kriegies" made plans for their future. They drew floor plans for the dream house they would build, chose motifs for the restaurant they would start—an astonishing number planned to open bars. Some wrote prospectuses for a business they would establish. One fellow outlined a motor-car race track he wanted to build on a piece of land he owned. Another—no doubt a hot pilot—intended to open a flying school and estimated costs for planes, hanger space, equipment, gas and oil, personnel, advertising and such.

Intricate plans, put down in thought-through detail, with no shortage of imagination. The only shortage was paper on which to draw plans.

Foolish dreams? Not for the planners. Only the future could tell how many visions were fulfilled, or even attempted, but all received an immediate reward—hope. One could notice a difference in morale between the prisoners who made plans and those who didn't. The planners were sustained by hope.

We all need a dream, something to work toward, to look forward to. Big dreams or small ones. Athletes set goals for the season and immigrants yearn to visit their homeland. A young man, or young woman, has always wanted to be president or a pilot. Some hanker to learn to ride a horse or play the piano. For seniors, there are before-I-die-I-want-to dreams. Mine are to visit Vermont in the autumn, to shoot my age on the golf course, attend a performance of Wagner's entire Ring Cycle at Bayreuth, and ride the Canadian National Railway coast to coast across the continent.

Goldie was a timid little housewife who kept a neat house, cooked fine meals for her family, raised her kids with total devotion, and lived in the shadow of her husband, Art. She never drove a car, never went to the movies because Art didn't want to go, read the paper after he had finished with it. But Goldie harbored a secret desire—to paint.

Art suffered a heart attack in his early sixties and died. As soon as he was laid to rest, Goldie took lessons and learned how to drive, then signed up for painting classes at the Y. When my family visited her a few years later, we were shocked. The house was a mess: furniture askew, beds unmade, a week's worth of dishes stacked up in the kitchen sink. But hung on the walls, stacked against chairs, and scattered on the floor of every room and the stairway were paintings. Watercolors of happy clowns, polished apples, vases of flowers, lush landscapes. And Goldie was aglow. When we asked to buy some of her paintings, she couldn't believe it, shyly told us to take what we wanted. She didn't need the recognition of others; she was living her dream.

Dreaming is tough in these times. Career plans are made unreliable by the certain uncertainty of layoffs that come when the company we work for decides to restructure or we get old and expensive to keep on. We have to expect to make career changes up to nine times in a worklife.

In our changing society, leaders seem intent upon tearing down the old before building the new. The focus is on what we don't want, not on what we do want. It seems pointless to make plans.

Charles Farnsley, a remarkable man once mayor of Louisville, used to hold an unshakable belief that every person needs a lost cause. He started a small publishing endeavor called the Lost Cause Press to spread the notion that serving a cause without hope of success has its rewards. Even the impossible dream has value.

Millions of us have not given up dreaming. Almost anyone who plays the lottery has spent hours surreptitiously planning how to spend the money if we hit the jackpot. Even if we never win, it's good practice, stretches the imagination—and tells us a lot about ourselves.

My dream for some years has been to have a place in the country, remote, with acres of woods, a lake or creek, and a picturesque old house, with modern conveniences, of course. I can tell you exactly what it would look like. A two-story windowed cupola rising from the corner of a long gingerbread-trimmed porch. My study would be on the second floor, looking over the expanse of unmowed meadow, planted in provender for birds, and the aspen trees lining the long lane from the road. The breakfast nook in the kitchen would have a large one-way window, with a bird feeder outside, so I could drink my coffee and read my morning newspaper and watch the birds having their breakfast.

Most of the land would be untillable, but on a few acres of what was, it would be no trick to put in tees and greens for a rude two-hole practice golf course. The land would be sown and kept as a haven for wildlife. Migrating ducks might stop at the pond, and some might stay. I'd fence the place, more for keeping in than keeping out, because of the animals—dogs, cats, squirrels, deer, coon, rabbits and such other critters who cared to take up residence—within limits, naturally.

I'd deed the place to the Nature Conservancy for perpetual use as a wildlife sanctuary. It is not an unlikely venture; there are places like that around, close by.

One can get carried away with visions and dreams. I got to wondering if a community dream was possible. Could people get together and ask "What kind of town do we want this to be?" and create a collective vision? Not something devised by a planning commission or consulting firm, or even political leaders. Not what we are against, but what we are for. More than economic development or preserving the past. A vision of how we want to live together, to commune with each other, to be a community.

It is not easy pulling people together around a vision, but it can happen. As an example of how some idle chit-chat turned into a vision that became a reality I offer riverfront development in Madison.

One evening some years ago at Mary's porch time, a few of us were watching the cars go by on Vaughn Drive and lamenting that there was no path on the riverbank where one could walk, jog, ride a bike, or run a dog.

In no time Mary, ever the doer, had pulled together a group to talk about building a walkway along the riverfront. There were six of us, our district councilman the only one with any official status. We bantered about plans, toured the riverbank, looked into property ownership. We agreed that the walk should be separated from vehicular traffic, by a lane or a wall. I favored a miniature version of the Atlantic City boardwalk, with overlook bays.

Before we had met twice, word of our scheming was leaked to the mayor. Wary of citizens taking matters into their own hands, he quickly formed a large riverfront committee, appointed a chairman, and subsumed us. No matter, the more the better.

Our first meetings were standard fare for community action: dredging up all the obstacles that would prevent us from accomplishing anything, suggestions that we hire a consultant and draw up a master plan. Once past these dysfunctional notions, we floundered.

Then I heard of charettes being held around the state by architectural students of Ball State University. A charette is a planning process that draws everybody involved in a proposed project for a marathon of meetings over several days, concluding with a consensus plan in which all have participated.

The committee jumped at the idea. Ball State agreed to send graduate students, faculty members and a landscape specialist. Mary carried the load of the considerable arrangements for their visit. They came, spent days talking with citizens and touring the town, nights sketching ideas for developing our riverfront, an unimproved asset that inspired the visitors.

The climax of the charette was a public meeting at the library auditorium, which overflowed, people standing outside trying to hear the presentation. The auditorium walls were covered with drawings, fascinating renditions of what could be done. More ideas emerged from the specialist's talk and the discussion after, such as selling memorial bricks to finance the walk.

A vision was taking hold.

The turnout and the talk about it, and surveys we did, showed that the riverfront was a part of people's lives and they were all for measures to make the most of it.

The charette came in the midst of a mayoralty campaign. After the outpouring of support for improving "Madison's front yard," the two candidates, silent on the subject before, began speaking of their lifelong devotion to the riverfront and their consuming resolve to see it developed to its ultimate potential.

Today, that casual vision of a path for dog walking and bike riding is almost a reality. Not quite what was originally envisioned, more of a drive-to, sit-and-look resting place than a walker's walk. And worshippers of the sacred car have had their way, again, in parking spaces up against the walk, bumpers overhanging. And benches close by, so that drivers exhausted by the 15-foot trip from car to walk can collapse and rest. Bike riders are seldom seen, probably banished by the ordinance against riding bikes on sidewalks. Lots of sauntering, though, and hanging out, even picnicking.

Nevertheless, Madison's long-and-lengthening stretch of memorial brick walk, flowered bays, plaza and gazebo, overlook and old-time street lights make it arguably the most usable, attractive river frontage of any city, large or small, for hundreds of miles up and down the river.

And stands as an enduring reminder of what citizens can do with a dream.

My dream of a refuge in the country was provoked by my run-ins with lawn lovers and enforcers of the let-no-animal-stray edict. At times it seemed to me like a conspiracy, exaggeration maybe, but conspiracy theories are popular nowadays. Madison's small-town sweetness soured quickly for me and I wanted to escape. Retreat to where my dogs and I would be safe from human predators.

That was in the era of the traveling triumvirate of Amigo, Sandy and George. Now it is just Squeaky and me.

He's been with me four years now and I still can't touch him. He sneaks up for a sniff but if I reach out my hand, he's gone. He'll sleep on my bed, until I turn in, then he jumps off and heads upstairs.

That's in warm weather, when the house is usually cooler than outdoors. In cold weather, he prefers to sleep out in the doghouse, which I've furnished with straw and braid rugs and he has arranged into a snug nest against the back wall that still gives him a watchdog view out the door.

It's me who gets concerned when the temperature drops into the teens or below. Too frigid to leave the door open for him to come in if he wants, so we have a system. I go out with a flashlight, flash it into the doghouse to see if he's there and ask if he wants to come in. Sometimes he does, but he waits a few minutes to establish that coming in is his own idea. He may refuse three or four invitations, 15 minutes apart. Finally, I come in grumbling, "Well, if that's the way he wants it. . ." Then I go to bed and feel guilty about being warm.

Occasionally he'll sleep across the street in Mary Ella's yard. Since she became a widow and lives alone she appreciates his protection. And he does protect. He's not a casual barker so when I hear him bark or howl, I know something's out there. A couple mornings ago I found the freshly killed carcass of a huge ground hog over there.

He has warmed up to me, within limits—his limits. Like every domesticated dog, going for a walk is what he lives for. He comes after me when it's time, and can sit there staring, putting the pressure on, until I relent. In the yard starting out, that's the only time he shows excitement. He'll play a bit then, although he's still not sure about me pretending to chase him. He rarely takes off on his own without me, odd after his years of straying.

We're communicating better, too. When he ranges out of sight on our trips and I can't remember if he's behind me or ahead, he'll use that squeak of his to let me know where he is. He'll stop and go at street crossings when I do, usually. Otherwise, I trust to his street skills although there have been times when he survived because a driver slowed down for him. To such drivers, he and I offer our gratitude.

Lately he's taken to reversing our customary routes, and can be doggedly independent about insisting on his way. As to who wins out most, it's a wash.

This little black stray dog has come to be kind of a symbol

for me, of something wrong in our society.

Squeaky has never bitten anyone (none of my dogs ever has). He's afraid of people, will run away if they get too close. He never barks without good reason. His status as a stray was determined by humans who dumped him and his sister off out on the highway. He's a victim, not a threat. No wonder he always has that grim, guarded look.

Yet his presence among us is regarded as a menace, prompts some people to reach for a phone or a gun. The woman who shot and killed Squeaky's sister, and shot and wounded him, could be described as perfectly within her rights and she no doubt believed she was performing a service.

Dogs are the only creatures that humans systematically destroy, every day, in every community. In Madison, we destroy about 600 dogs and 300 cats a year.

Were they a genuine hazard? Rabies is rare; dog bites occur, but often after provocation and the threat is frequently exaggerated.

Yes, there's a better solution—spaying, neutering and adoption. And many caring volunteers work tirelessly, with few funds, at this solution. Our tax money is spent to hunt down, round up, and destroy these victims.

It has been said that a civilized society is one which cares for its least fortunate members. A society that deals with its less fortunate by killing them is barbaric.

Squeaky is a maverick who is unknowingly trying to beat the system. So far, he has succeeded, but who knows?

So I say: Long Live Squeaky!

# Epilogue

About a year after I moved to Madison, I was offered an excellent job back in Washington, D.C., where I'd lived before. I wasn't even tempted then, I wrote in a magazine article at the time, but "time will tell if I was right or wrong."

Now, more than a decade later, I can say I was right. Move back to the big city? Never. Even visiting one bothers me—all the traffic congestion, taking so long to get anywhere, the crowds, even riding elevators bugs me.

Was Madison the right choice among the other places I considered before moving? Hard to say. Did Madison stand up over time to the criteria I set in my search for the best place for me? Of the 14 criteria (described in the Prologue), I would say Yes to 12, No to two of them.

On some points, Madison exceeded my expectations. The Library, for instance. I'm not the only one who appreciates its offerings, accommodating librarians and handsome building. Last year, readers in this small town checked out 144,986 books, thousands more magazines, books on tape, videocassettes, and reels of microfilm! One day they were standing five deep in three lines waiting to check out books. Who said reading is dead?

Sunrise Golf Course not only gets high marks from me, but from my dogs, for the rabbit-rich hunting ground it is on off hours. The Country Club course is also good for exploring, although I never played golf there.

One of my criteria was "a place to jog" and here Madison shines. Right outside my door is Vaughn Drive, two miles along the river for a testy four-mile workout from one end to the other and back. My preferred course is on the water's edge along the Kentucky side of the river, a stretch of more miles upriver than I need. Trouble is, it's often soggy or under water.

A running bonus I hadn't expected is the 10K Race the Saturday before the Regatta during Fourth of July week, sponsored by the Madison Courier and conducted with state-of-the-art efficiency.

It's a lovely course, easier on the eyes than the legs. Starts on the hilltop, runs a mile before you get out of the high-school parking lot, winds through the State Hospital grounds along a high bluff overlooking the river, a magnificent vista that may see hydroplanes on practice runs, rooster tails flying. Then through overhanging trees, out to a mile-long rush down Hanging Rock Hill past Springdale Cemetery and the drag along shaded Third Street to the finish. One year, I was first in the male over-70 category. Well, to be honest, I was the only one in that category and the fellow who usually wins it was out of town. Another year, I was the last man to finish; an ambulance followed me down the hill. It gets lonely back there so for next year I'm organizing a Back Pack, nonjocks who Run for Fun, Not for Fame. I've already had a t-shirt made with a caboose on the front and The End on the back.

One criteria not met was having "outlets for work in case I have to resort to honest labor." On this point, Madison is no different than any other town or city. The problem is age discrimination, one of the most virulent inequities in the land. Twenty years of applying for jobs that I was qualified for have taught me the standard unstated reasons for rejection: I'm overaged, overpriced, or overmatched. Anyone over 55 knows the script.

Although the appearance of a place was not one of my criteria, without question Madison's townscape influenced me in deciding to move here. And in my time here, the town's look has just gotten better. I'd argue that Madison is the best-looking town its size in the country. Some New England villages are picture pretty, but they are kept quaint more for visitors than for residents. Large cities, with all their resources and high-priced planning, seldom get beyond a gussied-up facade or a skyline impressive from a distance. For livable good looks, city limits to city limits, Madison is hard to match.

It's also a safe town. Oh, many residents don't think so and security systems are hot items. Crime on television scares us into believing that it is happening here, or might. We forget that news is the extraordinary, not the norm. One reason there's so much crime on the nightly news is that it's easy to cover, only takes a police scanner.

Talking over the fence with a neighbor, I remarked about how free of crime Madison was. "Oh, I don't know about that," he said, and told of having lawn chairs stolen right off his front porch. "When was that?" I asked. He thought a minute, then, "Must have been eight or nine years ago."

I only remember locking the door of my place once, when I was out of town. Don't even remember where the key is. Never lock my car. Of course, having dogs around makes a difference, as well as driving a car so old only a fool would steal it.

Convenience is another Madison plus. Nothing you want to get to is more than 10 minutes drive. I can get downtown in five minutes, walking. This is more than convenience, it's life giving. In the big city, I used up almost two hours of my life each work day commuting.

My major disappointment in Madison was in the "sense of community" I had hoped for. I was probably unrealistic, searching for the neighborliness of my childhood. Here I found some neighbors downright hostile, and even those who weren't agitated by my dogs didn't show me much welcome, spoke only when I did. Madison is not as friendly as it believes it is; friendly is Chamber of Commerce promotion, or extended by shopkeepers to tourists, or remarked upon by out-of-town newspaper or televison reporters who get an understandably warm reception. Just as many clerks in the stores are programmed to offer sterile have-a-nice-day courtesy as elsewhere, and show indifference and irritation when they get busy.

When I was a kid I knew everybody in our immediate neighborhood, had been in all of their houses but one. Here, I have seen the inside of precious few of the neighbors' homes. When a death occurred in the neighborhood I grew up in, everybody rallied around the grieving family. Women brought in cakes, pies, casseroles—then cooked and kept house for them. If Maxine, who lives down the block from me, doesn't collect for flowers when somebody in the neighborhood dies, it doesn't get done.

One day I noticed several cars parked around the townhouse across the alley. Later I found out the man who lived there had died. I'd chatted with him often, see his place out my study window constantly, yet he had died and I never knew it. Shook me a little.

One night walking down an alley with Squeaky I encountered a man cleaning out the trunk of his car. We got to talking. He had lived here all his life and told me, with clear disappointment, about how the town had changed. "It's just not the town it used to be," he said.

No small town is. We cling to the image of a community, as Madison was recently described, with "a warm fuzzy feeling." But that feeling is disappearing, or gone. Even Andy Griffith said, in an interview on a retrospective of his show, my all time favorite, "There is no Mayberry."

We don't need each other the way we once did. Certainly

not for entertainment. High technology has brought us everything we could want, coming out of that square box there in the
living room. So we hole up in our self-sufficient cocoons and it
takes a flood or earthquake to stir up a sense of community.

Madison is no better or worse than other small towns in that
respect. Even so, as we like to say about democracy being flawed
but still the best system of government, small towns are still the
best to come home to.

## About the illustrator

Steve Eberhardt is a free lance artist, sculptor, and graphics designer. After graduating in fine arts from the University of Evansville in Indiana, he spent two years in England painting portraits and another two years traveling the United States as an itinerant caricaturist. He now lives in Louisville, Kentucky with his wife Sue, a craftswoman and daughter of the author. They have painted scores of murals in schools and homes, a library, shopping malls, business firms and parking garages.

## The perfect, personal gift...

...for anyone who loves dogs or small towns

Send a copy of

**Where the grass is greener and dogs had better keep off**

...inscribed to the recipient's dog and autographed by the author.

Write your inscription below for each gift copy, with name and address to which each book should be sent:

_____

_____

_____

_____

_____

_____

_____

_____

_____

_____

_____

_____

_____

_____

_____

_____

_____

_____

_____

Tear out this page and mail to Limited Editions, Box 258, Milton, KY 40045, with check for $17.50 for each copy ordered ($14.95 book price, $2.55 special handling). Make check payable to Limited Editions.